THE REFERENCE SHELF VOLUME 34 NUMBER 1

THE OUTLOOK FOR YOUTH

EDITED BY ALICE H. HOROWITZ

THE H. W. WILSON COMPANY
NEW YORK 1962

THE REFERENCE SHELF

The books in this series reprint articles, excerpts from books, and addresses on current issues, social trends, and other aspects of American life, and occasional surveys of foreign countries. There are six separately bound numbers in each volume, all of which are generally published in the same calendar year. One number is a collection of recent speeches on a variety of subjects; each of the remaining numbers is devoted to a single subject and gives background information and discussion from varying points of view, followed by a comprehensive bibliography.

Subscribers to the current volume receive the books as issued. The subscription rate is $10 ($12 foreign) for a volume of six numbers. The price of single numbers is $2.50 each.

Library of Congress Catalog Card No. 62-9025

PRINTED IN THE UNITED STATES OF AMERICA

PREFACE

This volume, like others in the Reference Shelf series, is written primarily for a youthful audience. More than others, perhaps, it is directed specifically to these readers.

The articles in the first three sections deal with subjects of major importance to young people—education, employment, and marriage. It is hoped that the articles will serve as guidelines to help readers approach these vital areas with forethought and with an understanding of some of the problems involved.

More today than ever before, the influence—for good and for bad—of youth as a distinct group is felt in our society. The concluding section, "Present Trends," offers some general comments on the attitudes of high school and college students and outlines several ways in which young Americans have participated in public affairs in their own country and abroad.

The editor wishes to thank the authors and publishers who have courteously granted permission to reprint copyright materials in this book.

ALICE H. HOROWITZ

January 1962

NOTE TO THE READER

The following Reference Shelf compilations give further information on educational questions: *Educational Opportunities for Youth,* edited by Walter M. Daniels (Volume 27, Number 5); *America's Educational Needs,* edited by Grant S. McClellan (Volume 30, Number 5); and *Federal Aid to Education,* edited by Ronald Steel (Volume 33, Number 4).

CONTENTS

IV. Present Trends

I. EDUCATION

EDITOR'S INTRODUCTION

Between three and four million students are now attending colleges in the United States and many more apply than are accepted. Tensions which result from running the "college admissions race" are notorious. Yet, despite their eagerness to enter college, a large number of young people fail to exercise sufficient care in selecting the school at which they will have some of the most important experiences of their lives. In the first article in this section, Gordon Greer, an associate editor of *Better Homes & Gardens*, outlines the steps which a student should take to ensure that his choice of school is the right one. His analysis is based on research conducted by the National Merit Scholarship Corporation, which since 1955 has annually awarded some five hundred to one thousand four-year grants to high school seniors who excel in its national competitive examination. The NMSC administers funds donated by the Carnegie Corporation and the Ford Foundation, as well as by an increasing number of industrial firms.

Students thinking of applying to state colleges should note the admissions policies of these institutions, discussed in the second selection by R. Grann Lloyd of North Carolina College at Durham. As he points out, not all state colleges accept applicants from high schools within their respective states regardless of academic standing.

Indeed, the competition for college places, particularly at the few schools highest in public favor, is now very keen. Paradoxically, however, many institutions which offer a good education are unable to amass a full student body simply because they are less well known and do not receive enough applications. Two centers which act as coordinating agents for colleges seeking candidates and for students who need assistance in gaining college entrance are the College Admission Center, North Shore Hotel, Chicago, Illinois; and the College Admissions Assistance Center, 41 East 65th Street, New York 21, New York.

A glance at most college catalogs will show that the costs of higher education have risen tremendously within the last few years. Many colleges today charge from $700 to $1,500 annual tuition. "How To Pay for College," from *Changing Times,* details several ways in which the student and his family can plan to meet these costs. (For further reference the reader may consult *Need a Lift?* This excellent publication, which lists career facts and scholarship sources, as well as information on state laws concerning educational benefits, is published by the Education and Scholarship Committee of the American Legion.)

For the student who cannot or does not want to attend a four-year college, the next article, also from *Changing Times,* describes other kinds of schools which provide good post-high school education. "Education for Technicians" outlines more specifically the technical programs available, while "Other Educational Resources" cites learning opportunities available for those who must go to work directly after high school.

Unfortunately 20 to 40 per cent of the students now enrolled in high school will not even complete that course. Many of these will eventually discover the disadvantage of being unskilled in an increasingly complex technological society. The last selection outlines the nature of the high school dropout problem and appeals to schools to combat it.

HOW NOT TO PICK A COLLEGE HAPHAZARDLY [1]

The techniques now employed by high school students for picking the wrong colleges to attend are so efficient that 60 per cent of the freshmen who reach campus this autumn will either transfer or quit before graduating. This is the result, in large part, of two common misconceptions. First is the notion that colleges can be listed by reputation or popularity, as though they were tunes on the Hit Parade. Second is the nearly opposite assumption that colleges are all pretty much the same, so the choice might as well be dictated by convenience. One way is like proposing to a Hollywood star you've never met—and the other like making the same offer to the first girl you pass on the street.

[1] Article by Gordon Greer, associate special features editor of *Better Homes & Gardens,* based on research conducted by the National Merit Scholarship Corporation, 1580 Sherman Ave., Evanston, Ill. *Better Homes & Gardens.* 38:106+. O. '60. Reprinted by permission.

Yet even among the most promising students, only a few seem willing to believe that selecting a college calls for considerable reflection. In a report on its own crop of award winners, the National Merit Scholarship Corporation recently came to the conclusion that even the brightest young men and women are frequently guilty of making poor decisions.

In Pittsburgh, a similar survey has showed that of five hundred high school seniors there, each of whom had already selected the college he planned to attend, barely 10 per cent were even vaguely familiar with their chosen school's curriculum. Nearly 90 per cent had picked a college whose courses they knew nothing about!

If this sad situation is to be improved, it will call for a change of attitude. Only after they accept the distinction between colleges and commodities, and begin judging the former less casually, can students realistically expect to end up on a suitable campus.

For one thing, this would mean starting earlier. Though we are amused by the overzealous father who tries to enroll a year-old son at his alma mater, we should really feel sad about the high school graduate who goes into the summer before seeking a college for the fall. By that time, the choice is usually made on the basis of nothing more substantial than two or three evenings spent leafing through catalogs, many of which are misleading.

Anyone who decides to go to college at all should sign up in high school for "solid" courses: mathematics, history, science, English, ancient and foreign languages. The practice recently noted among college admissions officers of studying more carefully their applicants' extracurricular achievements is no sign of softening entrance requirements. In every case, these men make certain that extracurricular pursuits are just that; they must always be offered in addition to, never merely as a substitute for, solid academic accomplishment.

There are more than two thousand colleges and universities flung across America, and according to Merit Corporation research, these schools "differ tremendously." Finding the right one—or two or three, if you want to improve your chances for acceptance—takes longer than just a few evenings. It also involves more than comparing institutions. A major part of the project, in fact, is the matter of self-assessment. No college is good for everyone. The trick is to find one that's suitable for *you,* and this depends on your personality, your interests, your ability, and your pocketbook.

It's unlikely that many young men or women, told to evaluate themselves in those terms or to judge what career they might do best in, could do so with any certainty. More often than not, they need outside assistance—which in most communities is available more frequently than it's asked for.

High school counselors, though not consistently as helpful as educators might like to see them, usually have worth-while opinions to offer. They do best, of course, with students they know personally. But even when a student is no more than a name to him, the counselor has access to revealing records. Naturally, he has the student's grades and his teachers' estimates of his attitude and potential. Equally important, he has the records of previous students who entered (or failed to) any number of colleges, with later reports on how well they succeeded there. If the counselor knows how academic standards have changed, he can then predict with some confidence, using those earlier case histories for comparison, what a given student might reasonably accomplish at various schools and in various fields. Furthermore, he can give aptitude tests—usually free or at little cost—designed to gauge the depth of a student's interests and to help bring to light an appropriate career.

Other sources of outside counsel—parents, teachers, friends now in college, anyone with experience in a particular career—often prove equally helpful. Another useful source may be the college admissions officer. But remember that his primary job is to pick a freshman class, not to provide professional guidance. Don't contact an admissions officer until *after* deciding that a certain college interests you. Of course, if the admissions officer contacts *you,* or visits the local high school, that's another matter.

Even the student who can say with some certainty that his interests just haven't crystallized, already knows two things about what college to attend. First, its curriculum should not be specialized. Caltech [California Institute of Technology] and MIT [Massachusetts Institute of Technology], for example, are fine schools for future scientists and engineers but anyone with doubts about his profession would probably be better off somewhere else, preferably at a liberal arts school where a variety of subjects are available for sampling. Second, and not so obvious, the school should be of sufficient size to accommodate students who, *after* enrolling, display an interest in some specialty. This means a college with many departments or a university with several schools. Otherwise, to follow new interests, a student might have to change campuses, and transfer students, even more so than freshmen, can have a hard time getting admitted.

Obviously, more positive convictions make the problem easier. If a young man wants to be an engineer, has excellent grades in mathematics, a high mechanical aptitude, a suitable temperament, and adequate desire, there's no sound reason why he needs to consider anything other than an engineering college.

The important point, in either case, is this: Assessing the student's abilities and interests should precede the search for an appropriate school. Always, forever, and without exception, pick the college to suit the person. Never go at it any other way.

Once a candidate thinks he has a good line on himself, any of several college guides . . . can indicate which schools warrant consideration. Young men or women undecided about their courses of study might extract from these lists scores of possibilities. Others, with more definite ambitions, can narrow the choice to a smaller number. Then, with this first screening out of the way, it's time to start reading catalogs.

Anyone who rejects what sounds like hoopla and concentrates on specific facts can be helped by catalogs. The obvious is important: Size of the school, its geographic setting, the ratio of female students to male, whether or not there are fraternities or sororities, the existence of any religious support, housing and eating accommodations, tuition fees and living expenses—all these factors should be carefully weighed. They have nothing to do with academic quality, but can mean the difference between a student's happiness and despair. From the Merit Scholarship files come examples which show that one young man, the product of a small western town, was recently transferring from an Ivy League college because "the pace of eastern living is one to which I cannot adjust," while another, this one an Easterner, was moving out of a small-town school because "I find that the greatest percentage of the time I am, in a word, bored."

Depending on personal circumstances, there are other things a student wants to know that a catalog can tell him. Young men can learn about ROTC—whether it's required or available, and if so, what branch of the military is involved. Students with a record of superior grades can see which colleges grant early admission to unusually qualified high school juniors (thus sparing them the senior year rush and tumble), and which schools admit a few outstanding freshmen under various "advanced status" programs.

A certain percentage of the future college crowd might also have an interest in money. Arthur Fleming, [former] Secretary of the Department of Health, Education, and Welfare, recently noted that a college education is just about a third more expensive today than it was only four years ago, and furthermore, that a similar increase is expected in the next four years. Obviously, more students than ever will need financial assistance. College catalogs sometimes indicate where it might (or might not) lie.

They mention it, for instance, when a school participates in the National Defense Student Loan Program (at last count, 1,360 colleges did), in which case its students can qualify for low-interest Federal loans. Any scholarships or loans from the college itself are also outlined in its catalog, and sometimes information is offered on the subject of part-time work. (Of course, there are other sources of financial help seldom mentioned in these publications—state and local governments, for instance, various private organizations, and a number of fraternal groups.)

Material culled from catalogs can also reflect scholastic quality—though it usually takes a little interpreting. All schools, for example, speak prominently about "superior teaching" and "great academic scope." But you should read the smaller type before you accept such claims. Specifically, there are four good signs that a college is less than scholastically perfect:

First, if it offers only a limited number of courses. Obviously, any college—or any single department—which covers inadequately its field of concentration is at a definite disadvantage.

Second, if there are too few teachers. No matter how excellent an instructor may be, students, especially in their fields of special interest, should enjoy a wide variety; no history major wants to learn all his history from a single point of view.

Third, if the teachers, however many, are graduates of only a handful of schools. Good colleges try to pick their staffs from a wide academic background. If a large percentage of a college's teachers come from the same few institutions—especially if that small number of colleges includes the one now employing them—there's reason to hesitate before applying.

Fourth, if the doctorate ratio is low. Decorating his name with "Ph.D." doesn't necessarily make anyone a better teacher, but in the practical world of education, it does increase his salary, and for a college to hire just a few Ph.D.'s (the national average is roughly 40 per cent) is a sign that whoever controls the budget is not spending as much money on teachers as other colleges are. Despite this, the faculty may be good, but the odds are generally against it. (Yet famous names on the teaching staff, though they usually command high wages, shouldn't be given undue importance. Much of their salary derives from publicity—famous professors are good drawing cards—and frequently they teach only one or two classes, sometimes no classes at all. In judging how well a teacher stimulates students, according to Merit Corporation research, "capacity for human relations is often more important than professional distinction.")

Such, then, are the things a student can figure out from reading and comparing catalogs. What he *can't* get from any catalog is a true grasp of a college's atmosphere—its unique set of elusive characteristics that amount almost to a personality. Yet this, too, is something to be carefully considered.

Students in the natural sciences, for instance, seem to prosper in one type of environment while those in the arts and humanities do better in quite another. Reduced to its starkest simplicity, the Merit analysis indicates that the climate for sciences is quite demanding ("The school tries very hard to flunk you out," as one young scholar put it), while a broader, more permissive atmosphere seems best for the arts and humanities ("If a student fails a course he can usually substitute another one for it rather than take it over").

Sociologist David Riesman has suggested that since no student can possibly find out for himself all he ought to know about even *one* college, let alone half a dozen or more, there should be a consumer research bureau like those now established for such commodities as vacuum cleaners and dry goods, in which unbiased experts would roam the countryside studying and evaluating colleges, then publish their conclusions for the guidance of the young. But so far, this project hasn't made much headway, and students must rely on their own devices.

One way they've found to learn more about a college is to go there and look it over. Often this is a good idea. But other times such trips cost too much, or the young men or women arrive unprepared; they don't know what they're supposed to look for, or where they'd be likely to find it, so they wander aimlessly over the campus, admiring the scenery and seeing little else. Such wastefulness is unnecessary. By dropping a note beforehand to the Dean of Admissions, nine times out of ten a student can arrange for a personal tour to see just what happens on a typical college day. (By all means, he should avoid the mistake of going during the summertime, on a weekend, or on Visiting Day.) He can sit in on classes, talk with professors, tour the dorms and cafeterias, sample some of the social life, and generally preview those things he'd be doing as a freshman at that institution.

Talking with college students home on vacations is another useful device, as is visiting a local alumni chapter. And sometimes the Dean of Men (or Women) will answer questions posed in a letter.

When the time comes for making final applications, the three-college parlay is probably the best technique. Applying to more than three schools can be expensive (though anyone who can afford it will be that much better off), and to fewer than three can be dangerous.

The two top choices should be made without restrictions, then a third purely for insurance. The last is a college which, for various reasons, is almost certain to grant admission. This need not mean a second-rate institution. It might be a state university where entrance requirements are kept low by law; it might be the family alma mater (many colleges give priority to children of their alumni); or it might be a college that's geographically remote, trying to include in its freshman class more students from other parts of the country.

Pressure and payola will get you nowhere. Unsolicited testimonials, especially from people with famous names or political importance, are apt to count *against* a candidate. All colleges tell their applicants precisely what needs to be done—what records to file, what tests to take, how much money to send along. Each of these chores should be carried out. Beyond that, all any student can do is go to church regularly, lead a clean life, keep his fingers and toes crossed, and pray.

ADMISSION POLICY IN STATE-SUPPORTED HIGHER EDUCATION [2]

Admission policies extant in American institutions of higher learning are many, varied, and complex. It would be unwieldly and well-nigh impossible to deal with all or most of them in a single study. Moreover, there is the persistent question of differences in admission policies in private and public-supported higher education institutions. Hence, the writer conducted a study of a single aspect of admission policy in state-supported colleges and universities. The purpose of the study was to test the oft-repeated cliché that state-supported colleges and universities must accept any graduate of a high school within the state who makes application for admission.

To secure the data for this study, the writer directed an inquiry to the attorneys general of the 50 states, Puerto Rico, and the District of Columbia. . . . A 100 per cent response to the inquiry was received.

Whereas state-supported colleges and universities in only 11 or 22 per cent of the states are required to accept any graduate from a high school within its borders who makes application for admission without regard to mental aptitude or other factors, 39 or 78 per cent are not, but 10 or 20 per cent do so as a matter of policy. Furthermore, 7 (63.6 per cent) of the 11 states that require state-supported higher education institutions to accept any graduate of a high school within its borders who makes application for admission are ranked among the lower half of the states on the basis of population.

Not a single New England state requires state-supported colleges and universities to accept any graduate from a high school within its borders who makes application for admission, and not a single one does so as a matter of policy. In fact, the

[2] From article by R. Grann Lloyd, who teaches in the Department of Commerce, North Carolina College at Durham. *School and Society*. 88:446-7. N. 19, '60. Reprinted by permission.

data show that not a single eastern state requires state-supported higher education institutions to accept any graduate from a high school within the state applying for admission, and only Maryland does so as a matter of policy. The data indicate, too, that wholesale admission of applicants from high schools within a state is most frequent west of the Mississippi River.

Today there are forecasts of stiffer college examinations as part of a trend toward higher admission standards. However, as a practical matter, college entrance examinations probably mean very little. For example, the respondent from New Mexico asserted: "Each of our institutions reserves the right to require examinations for admission. As a practical matter, however, high school graduation is tantamount to college entrance." The respondent from Utah said:

It is the general policy of the state universities to require applicants to take an entrance examination. This examination is not generally used as a basis for granting or refusing admission. It is used primarily to determine the capacity of each student and thereby provide the faculty and the student advisers an index of what to expect of each individual student, and also provide information upon which a suitable program can be arranged for a particular student.

An Arkansas participant in this study corroborated our thesis: "While individual aptitude, mental ability and entrance tests are given, they are used for the purpose of grouping students together with similar ability rather than as a condition for admission."

Nevertheless, it is somewhat heartening to note that applicants for admission to the University of Maryland . . . [whose academic records fall below a specified standard] must take a series of tests. If the scores indicate a reasonable chance of success in college, admission on probation is granted. Those applicants who do not make a satisfactory score are denied admission and advised against attempting to do college work without further preparation. However, if a parent insists that an applicant in this last category be given a chance to try college work, he will be admitted but only on very strict probation and after the parent has signed a statement recognizing that the university has advised against enrollment in a college program.

The cardinal finding of this study seems to be that the cliché that state-supported colleges and universities must accept any

ADMISSION POLICY IN STATE-SUPPORTED COLLEGES AND UNIVERSITIES[a]

Required to Accept Any Graduate Within the State Without Regard to Mental Aptitude or Other Factors	Not Required to Accept Any Graduate of a High School Within the State Without Regard to Mental Aptitude or Other Factors		Not Required to Accept Any Graduate of a High School Within the State Without Regard to Mental Aptitude or Other Factors, but Do So as a Matter of Policy
1. Colorado	1. Arizona	15. Mississippi	1. Alaska
2. Idaho	2. Arkansas	16. Nebraska	2. Alabama
3. Kansas	3. California	17. New Hampshire	3. Illinois
4. Louisiana	4. Delaware	18. New Jersey	4. Indiana
5. Missouri	5. Connecticut	19. New Mexico	5. Maryland
6. Montana[b]	6. Florida	20. New York	6. Nevada[d]
7. North Dakota	7. Georgia	21. North Carolina	7. Oregon
8. Ohio	8. Hawaii	22. Oklahoma	8. Texas
9. Washington	9. Iowa	23. Pennsylvania	9. Utah
10. West Virginia[c]	10. Kentucky	24. Rhode Island	10. Wisconsin
11. Wyoming	11. Maine	25. South Carolina	
	12. Massachusetts	26. South Dakota	
	13. Michigan	27. Tennessee	
	14. Minnesota	28. Vermont	
	29. Virginia		

[a] Publicly supported colleges and universities in the District of Columbia and Puerto Rico are not required to accept any graduate of a high school within their borders who make application for admission without regard to mental aptitude or other factors.

[b] When the tabulated data were submitted to the respondents for review, the respondent for Montana emphasized that: "State-supported colleges and universities in Montana accept as applicants for admission, without regard to the individual applicant's mental aptitude or other factors, graduates of four-year high schools, or academies, *fully* accredited by the State Board of Education."

[c] Beginning in 1961, only applicants from the upper three-quarters of each high-school graduating class will be admitted to state-supported colleges and universities in West Virginia without examination.

[d] As a matter of comity, the University of Nevada, the only institution of higher learning in the state, accepts any graduate of a high school within its borders who makes application for admission without regard to the applicant's mental aptitude or other factors. Hence, the respondent asserts: ". . . it is assumed that [Nevada has] something of a moral responsibility to provide opportunities beyond high school for any resident of the state who can profit from the instruction which the resources of the University make possible."

graduate of a high school within the state who makes application for admission is repeated glibly and recklessly. It is hoped that the findings of this study will encourage restraint in its future use.

HOW TO PAY FOR COLLEGE [3]

There is so much talk these days about the high cost of college that many families—especially those with two or more students to support—tend to grow panicky. These important facts become obscured:

Sure, college can be extremely expensive. No sense hiding that. But there are many colleges—good ones—that are not expensive at all.

Even a costly institution needn't automatically be ruled out. If it's the right place for the student, he may be surprised to learn that a way can be found for him to go there.

Several changes have taken place in the methods by which college can be financed. Parents who think that the only way a youngster can afford to go is to "win a scholarship" or "work his way through" must adopt new attitudes.

Any student who qualifies for college can afford to go—if he really wants to and is willing to do some hard planning with his family.

The earlier planning begins, the easier the task. Ideally, families should begin saving for college just about as soon as a child is born. And students themselves ought to give serious attention to the money problem when they reach junior high school. Even if college is only a year or two ahead, however, you can swing it if you prepare systematically, taking the steps outlined below.

Which College?

Expenses vary with the type of college you attend. Your first move, then, if college is just ahead is to make some realistic choices. Even if you still have several years before you apply, you'd be wise to think about what type of college you'd want to attend, could be admitted to and could afford.

[3] Article reprinted by permission from *Changing Times*, the Kiplinger Magazine. 14:41+. S. '60.

Choose a range of places, half a dozen or so to begin with. Think mainly of quality—courses offered, academic atmosphere, special programs that interest you, reputation. Forget prestige. Do try to include some nearby colleges that you could attend while living at home and some public institutions where tuitions for local residents are low.

Remember that the price tag on an education does not measure its value. A free school near home may suit you far better than a prestige-laden college many miles away. Parents especially are too often drawn to the famous institutions out of a desire for social status or because they attended one in the days when costs were lower and admission was easier. The student who must in the end "settle for" a less well-known and less expensive school starts his college career in the doldrums instead of with high anticipation.

Don't list a college as a preference simply because it's cheap. There's no sense in attending a college that you won't like or find stimulating. You can always find some way to go to a college that does suit you.

Figure the Cost

Now make realistic estimates of expenses at each college on the list. See what the catalogs say. Put figures down for these items:

Tuition and fees; books and supplies; room; meals, snacks, cigarettes; dues; entertainment; health; clothing, laundry, dry cleaning; personal grooming; travel between home and school; travel while at school; other current expenses; capital expenditures, such as a typewriter, prorated annually.

Notice this about your estimates: Educational expenses—that is, tuition, fees, books and supplies—account for between one and two fifths of your total costs. The bulk of your expenses are for living, especially for these five items: room, board, clothes, travel, recreation.

For costs at colleges near home, do figure what food, clothing and commuting will come to. This will help you compare expenses fairly with other colleges.

If you are looking ahead several years, better add at least 5 per cent a year to your figures to get some idea of what future costs will be like. By 1970, college expenses may very likely be double what they are now.

Savings and Assets

Once you've pinned down costs, you can begin canvassing your resources, and the first place to look, of course, is at the bank book. Unfortunately, most families don't save for college. An Elmo Roper survey found that even among those who do, half put aside no more than $150 a year. At that rate it might take ten years to save up enough money for one year of college for one child.

Even that helps, though. Any amount of savings, added to other resources, can mean the difference between a student's going to the college of his choice or taking second best. Savings are accumulated in various ways: paid-up mortgages, paid-up insurance, business investments, bonds, stocks, etc. According to college officials, families have a tendency to look only at their savings accounts when college costs are contemplated, though they may have other substantial assets at hand.

How Much from Income?

Even if the family did start a savings program years ago, chances are that inflation has reduced its effectiveness. What can you afford out of current income? Think of the ordinary living expenses being borne by the family now: food, clothing, health costs, etc. Some of this money can be allocated to student support.

Face the fact that the family may have to pinch somewhere. Too many people automatically discard the notion that they can afford anything out of current income for education. . . . [Below] you will see what colleges generally expect you to be able to pay out of income for education.

Pay As You Go

You can spread out the costs of college on a monthly basis just as you do the cost of a car. New plans are springing up all the time.

For information about installment arrangements, get in touch with your college and inquire at your local bank. Also, write to these agencies:

The Tuition Plan, Inc., One Park Avenue, New York 16, New York.

Insured Tuition Payment Plan, 38 Newbury Street, Boston 16, Massachusetts.

Funds for Education, Inc., 319 Lincoln Street, Manchester, New Hampshire.

Education Funds, Inc., 10 Dorrance Street, Providence 3, Rhode Island.

Before you choose your plan, study several carefully and compare them on these points:

Costs. One group of banks charges you $15 to make an application. Others make no charge. In the case of one loan agency, an amount of $4,800 can be paid off over four years in monthly installments of $108.73. In another plan, the same amount is repaid in installments of $104.38.

In comparing costs, work out the amount actually borrowed and the amount actually repaid.

Eligibility. Some banks can make loans only to state residents. Some agencies make their loans through colleges. Others can serve you directly. Be sure the service you are considering is really available to you.

Insurance. Is the loan guaranteed if the parent dies or becomes totally disabled? What's the cost of the insurance? Is it included in the installment fees you've been figuring on?

Cancellation. Be certain that you can pay off your loan early or cancel it without penalty.

Look For a Long-term Loan

The plans listed above are short-term installment loans. You may be able to do better by borrowing for a long period. Look into these:

U.S. Government loans. You apply through your college. Here are the main terms:

You can borrow up to a total of $5,000 at 3 per cent on the unpaid balance. Neither interest nor repayment begins until one year after you finish or quit your studies, and you may take ten years.

You get preference if you're a top student heading for work in teaching, math, one of the sciences, engineering or a foreign language.

Although millions of dollars are available and a great many Federal loans are made, competition for them is high and you must be able to show that you need one. Each college works out its own way of judging financial need.

College loans. In addition to Federal funds, at least eight hundred colleges have their own loan programs. Interest rates run about 2 per cent or less—sometimes nothing—during college, 4 per cent or less afterward; and generally you get all the time you need to pay up.

State programs. Some states have plans that encourage banks to make long-term loans. In New York you can obtain a bank loan for repayment at 4 per cent to 6 per cent over six years after college; and in Massachusetts for repayment at 6 per cent (current prime rate) over three years after college. Check with the local banks.

Private loan funds. Many associations, companies, foundations, alumni clubs and other groups have set up loan funds. Ask your high school counselor about them.

Watch the newspapers for new loan funds. One foundation, for example, is planning a national version of the program started in Massachusetts. Under it, a student in any part of the country may soon be able to borrow up to $700 a year from his hometown bank at the prime commercial rate and pay it back over forty-two months after he leaves school. It it works out, this plan will make available as much as half a billion dollars for educational loans in the next few years.

Would you be wise to saddle yourself with a long-term debt? Some things that you should think about:

If a loan means the difference between going or not going to college, take it. It will pay for itself in increased lifetime income and, more important, in greater personal fulfillment.

If it helps you go to the college of your first choice, take it. The more enthusiastic you are about your school, the more you'll get out of it. But if the loan is simply helping you go to a costly place for the sake of the prestige, think it over. Maybe you'd do better at a nearby, less expensive college, without taking on a debt. The availability of the loan makes your choice a free one, based on what you want out of college, not on what it costs.

Plan To Earn

You can certainly earn some of your college expenses. Most students do. But you can't plan on earning all your expenses, or even the major part of them. Costs are too high and the competition for jobs, too tough. Here's what *Changing Times* found in a survey:

Men students average from $150 during the school year at some colleges to $800 or more at others. Women seldom average over $500.

Some typical hourly rates: food service worker—50 cents to $1.40; clerk-typist—50 cents to $1.50; lab assistant—50 cents to $1.50; retail clerk—65 cents to $2.

Jobs are harder to get at colleges in small towns and colleges in the South. They are easier to get if you have a special skill, such as typing, car repairing, playing an instrument.

Don't plan to work more than twenty hours a week, say most colleges, or you'll hurt your grades. If you need the money, take a loan.

You should be able to earn anywhere from $250 to $600 each summer, sometimes more.

Ask the college placement office for leads about jobs.

Can You Get a Scholarship?

That question pops into everyone's head the moment college is mentioned. Well, maybe you can—if you rank in the top third of your class, have test scores that show high promise, are outstanding in other ways, such as "leadership," can demonstrate strong motivation, and, finally, really need financial help.

If you win a scholarship, your need will govern the amount. That's defined as the difference between what college costs and what you and your family can pay toward that cost. Assuming that your parents have no large assets and no unusual burdens, here roughly is the amount of annual support expected from them if you live at school.

family income	number of dependent children in family 1	2	3	4	5
$ 2,000	$ 240	$ 185	$ 145	$ 120	$ 105
4,000	555	445	370	305	240
6,000	885	685	615	525	435
8,000	1,250	965	840	755	660
10,000	1,750	1,370	1,165	1,020	915
12,000	2,300	1,805	1,535	1,350	1,210

Your aid may come as a combination scholarship-loan-job. Biggest amounts are given at the famous private colleges, but they're the most costly, too, and competition is intense.

Investigate these sources for scholarships: your school counselor; the college; the state department of education; local industry and service clubs; any organizations your parents belong to; your church; veterans' groups if you are the child of a veteran.

Add up all your resources now—your estimates of what might be available from each—and match them against the colleges you've picked. If you have made a conscientious effort to pin down every possible source of help, you should find that you can afford a college that suits you.

IT DOESN'T HAVE TO BE A REGULAR FOUR-YEAR COLLEGE [4]

Much of the college talk you hear these days gives the impression that the only worth-while education after high school is at a regular four-year institution. Nothing could be further from the truth. Not everyone can, or should, spend four years at college; not everyone wants to.

Besides, there are plenty of other educational programs for the high school graduate to pick from. Some are free; others are as costly as regular college courses and very much like them in content, too. Some train for specific jobs; some permit a youngster to learn while he works. Some take a few months, some as long as three years. Most are available right in the student's own community. Here's a rundown of the choices.

[4] Article reprinted by permission from *Changing Times*, the Kiplinger Magazine. 15:36+. Jl. '61.

Junior Colleges

Every fourth student who continues his education after high school does so at a junior college. Some states expect that pretty soon as many as 50 per cent of their high school graduates who go on studying will want to go to a junior college.

Already there are . . . [over 650] two-year colleges. Some—like Stephens in Missouri, Briarcliff in New York, Pine Manor in Massachusetts—are nearly as famous as well-known four-year liberal arts colleges and about as hard to get into. The kind that's spreading most rapidly, though, is the free or inexpensive community college that you can attend while living at home.

Courses range from vocational training to liberal arts. At most schools you can choose between a program that will prepare you for transfer to a regular four-year college or a "terminal" program that is completed in two years.

The transfer, or "university parallel," curriculum is the equivalent of two years at a liberal arts college. It's a convenient program for a youngster who isn't sure he wants or can take a full four-year course. It's fine, too, for the student who has been turned down by a four-year college and needs a chance to prove himself. A couple of years ago about 2,500 junior college graduates entered the University of California. Half would not have been academically eligible as freshmen. Subsequently, 73 per cent graduated.

Is it tough to transfer? Not especially. True, the best-known colleges—Harvard, Yale, Amherst, and so on—take few upper-classmen. But most do have room, particularly the state universities that are encouraging the development of two-year colleges and—as in Illinois and Florida—are even establishing special scholarships for transfer students. . . .

The most distinctive feature of the junior college is its terminal course. That's the two-year curriculum at the end of which you may obtain an Associate in Arts or other Associate degree. Courses range from liberal arts to vocational and semiprofessional programs.

Here are some examples of offerings at two-year colleges:

1. Joplin Junior College in Missouri, a co-ed community college with day and evening classes. Fees: about $105 to $265.

Transfer programs include liberal arts and these preprofessional courses: agriculture, business, dentistry, engineering, law, medicine, music, nursing, pharmacy, teaching, veterinary science, journalism, social work.

Terminal programs include general education, building trades, auto mechanics, salesmanship, secretarial training, elementary teaching, woodworking, medical technology, nursing.

Degrees offered: Associate in Arts, Science, Business, Music, Education or Technology.

2. Endicott Junior College in Massachusetts, a private college for women. Fees—about $2,200, including room, board, tuition; about $800 for day students.

Transfer programs: liberal arts, home economics, music, nursing, teaching, medical technology, occupational therapy, physical therapy.

Terminal courses: general education; art; business; home economics; journalism; medical laboratory technology; legal, medical, foreign or executive secretarial training; salesmanship; merchandising; clothing and fashion design; kindergarten-nursery teaching; radio and TV production; advertising; photography; hotel, restaurant or institutional management; theatre arts; public relations.

Degrees: Associate in Arts or Science.

For information about junior colleges, write to the American Association of Junior Colleges, 1785 Massachusetts Avenue, N.W., Washington 6, D.C. . . .

Technical Institutes

One of the greatest occupational demands in the years just ahead will be for technicians, who now do much of the work once done by engineers and scientists. About fifteen thousand engineering technicians are graduated in this country each year. Experts say we will need at least thirty thousand by 1970. . . .

You can get technical training at a variety of places: junior colleges; privately owned schools; company-run training schools; government-supported schools. Any of these might qualify as a "technical institute"—that is, a school that specializes in one or more of the branches of engineering technology; aeronautics; air conditioning, heating and refrigeration; automotive, diesel and steam technologies; construction; chemical technology; civil engineering technology; electronics; instrument and watch making; mechanics and metallurgy; tool designing; draftsmanship; computer technology.

Courses run from one to three years, with two the most common. Some schools offer cooperative programs in which you hold a job part of the time, attend school part of the time. Night courses are available at many schools, too.

For admission to a technical institute you must be a high school grad and have a good record in mathematics through algebra and geometry. You ought to have mechanical and scientific aptitudes, too. If you qualify, getting into a technical institute isn't difficult, for most have plenty of room for additional students right now and are planning to expand, besides.

Tuition costs range from nothing or a nominal fee at some publicly supported institutes to $900 or so a year at some privately run schools.

Here are fees and programs at typical institutes:

Broome Technical Community College, Binghamton, New York. $300 to $600. Courses in chemical, electrical, mechanical technologies.

Ohio College of Applied Science, Cincinnati, Ohio. $450 to $700. Chemical, electrical and electronic technologies; mechanical engineering technology.

Wentworth Institute, Boston, Massachusetts. $655, not including room and board. Aircraft maintenance technology; architectural engineering technology; building construction technology; civil and highway engineering technology; electrical engineering technology (electronic or power); mechanical engineering technology (design or heat power); metals engineering technology; production engineering technology.

A list of technical institutes accredited by the Engineers' Council for Professional Development is available . . . from the Council at 345 East 47th Street, New York 17, New York.

You can obtain a free list of schools approved by the National Council of Technical Schools by writing to them at Room 103, 1507 M Street, N.W., Washington 5, D.C.

Vocational Schools

Scattered through all parts of the country are some four thousand vocational training schools operated by private individuals, trade associations, hospitals and companies. Courses run anywhere from a few weeks to several years and cover just about any vocation you might think of.

At the Taylors Trade School in Chicago you can learn dress designing and tailoring in a twenty-seven-week course, thirty hours per week, for $150.

At the Washington School for Secretaries in the District of Columbia you can take a one-year secretarial course for about $700.

For $750 and up you can have an eighteen-week course in chick sexing at the American Chick Sexing Association School in Lansdale, Pa.

At any one of some five hundred approved schools, mostly run by hospitals, you can learn to be an X-ray technician at no tuition. In fact, you may get free laundry service and a stipend besides.

At other schools you can learn acting, auto repair, barbering, police work, dressmaking, mortuary science, cosmetology, advertising, dancing, upholstering, welding, modeling, selling, dairy farming, diamond cutting, etc. . . .

Free Vocational Courses

You can get excellent free training in a high-demand skill under Federal and state vocational programs. Daytime and evening courses are given at local high schools, two-year colleges, technical institutes and other special schools.

Here are some of the subjects offered: electronics; mechanical drafting; tool design; instrumentation; industrial chemistry; data programing; metallurgy; tool optics; missile telemetry; servomechanisms; radar theory; automation electronics; microwave theory; theory of transistors; electronic data processing; stress analysis; technical report writing; cost analysis; time study; quality control; tool planning.

In addition, many local schools systems, with the help of local businessmen, are developing post-high school cooperative courses in what is called "distributive education." In these programs you divide your time about equally between study and work in your special field. Training is given in a variety of business activities: advertising, construction, insurance, real estate,

financial services, transportation, retail and wholesale selling, warehousing, etc.

Inquire about these programs at your local or state school departments.

On-the-job Training

You may be able to qualify for training as an apprentice in one of the skilled trades. Master craftsmen teach you. You start at no less than half full-scale wages and are given regular increases, usually every six months. At the end of the program you receive full wages and are accepted into the craft union of your trade. Conditions of the job and the training course are all worked out under Federal regulations.

More than ninety different skilled trades offer apprentice programs. Getting into them isn't easy. You must have above average aptitude for the trade, be able to pass a physical test—and, of course, there must be an opening. A few of the occupations with estimated training periods:

automotive mechanic	3-4 years
butcher-meatcutter	3 years
carpenter	4 years
electrotyper	5-6 years
jeweler	3-4 years
printer	5-6 years
farm equipment mechanic	3-4 years

For information get in touch with your state employment service, your state apprenticeship council or the Department of Labor, Bureau of Apprenticeship and Training, Washington 25, D.C.

Many large companies have training programs that are not officially apprenticeship programs but that do move the trainee through systematic schooling while he's on the job.

Pitney-Bowes, Inc., manufacturer of mailing machines, offers a four-year work-training program in machine design to high school graduates with good records in algebra, trigonometry and mechanical drawing. Besides receiving on-the-job instruction, the trainee attends the Bridgeport Engineering Institute at company expense. At the end of the course he receives an Associate degree in machine design.

International Business Machines Corporation, which, among other things, makes electronic office machines and computers, gives courses that last from a few months to three years and cover such fields as toolmaking, machining, electronics, model making, automation techniques, customer engineering.

On-the-job training programs are available in many large companies in these fields: electricity and electronics; aircraft; automobiles; steel; oil refining. For information about a field that particularly interests you, write to companies in that field.

Other Opportunities

Even if you simply take a job after high school, you can continue your education.

About 140 colleges run evening classes. For a list of them write to the Executive Secretary, Association of University Evening Colleges, Brooklyn College, Brooklyn 10, New York.

Home study courses are okay, if you really work at them. Hundreds are available at from $25 to $500 a year. For information about private correspondence schools write to the National Home Study Council, 2000 K Street, N.W., Washington 6, D.C. . . .

Which School?

Here are some guidelines for choosing a post-high school program:

Be sure the field you go into suits your aptitudes and interests. Don't fall for school ads that promise you a career in a field that may not be right for you.

If you're going to a vocational, technical or preprofessional school, be certain that it's approved by the professional organization in the field you're aiming for.

Watch out for "diploma mills"—schools that offer quick degrees for a price. Check with your state or local education authorities about any school you go to.

One last suggestion: Don't enter any educational program unless you intend to give it a hard try. Jumping from school to school won't help you. Make some investigations about the school—and about your own needs—first.

EDUCATION FOR TECHNICIANS [5]

Shortages of Technicians

The shortages of professional workers, especially engineers, during World War II contributed to the rapid growth of technical and related semiprofessional occupations. Technicians, with one to three years of intensive and practical college-level training, performed many of the tasks that had been assigned to professional engineers. They filled many new jobs created by new methods of manufacture.

Surveys conducted during the latter part of the war showed that of all supervisory and technical workers in a representative group of manufacturing plants, only 0.8 per cent were graduates of technical institutes and 13.0 per cent were college graduates. For industry as a whole, the need was for a ratio of about five technical school trained workers to every engineering graduate.

In specific industries, the desired ratio of technicians per engineer ranged from 2.0 in hydroelectric development, to 20 technicians per engineer in wood processing. In between were iron and steel with 6 technicians needed for each engineer; metal products, 8.0 technicians; rail transportation, 9.1; telegraph and telephone communications, 9.7; textile manufacturing, 9.8; electrical manufacturing, 10.0; pulp and paper manufacturing, 10.3; and shipbuilding, 13.6. It may be some time before industry is able to achieve this desired ratio because of the limitation in training facilities for technicians.

Technical Occupations

Workers trained in technical institutes and in other schools offering technical programs of less than four years qualify for such jobs as laboratory technician, tester, junior designer, inspector, estimator, expediter, production supervisor, engineering aide, etc.

A brief definition of technical institute programs may help you better to understand them. These programs are intermediate between the high school and the vocational school on one hand,

[5] From *Careers for Technical School Graduates.* B'nai B'rith Vocational Service Bureau. 1640 Rhode Island Ave. N.W. Washington 6, D.C. '52. Reprinted by permission.

and the engineering school on the other. They are designed to prepare you for positions that are auxiliary to, but not in the field of, professional engineering. The courses lean heavily to the sciences and include the study of mathematics beyond the high school level. The courses are briefer, more intensive and more specific in purpose than professional engineering courses. Students are prepared for specific technical positions. Technical institutes generally don't train students for skilled trades.

A large number of schools offer not only full-time programs, but also evening and other part-time classes, and part-time co-operative training arrangements. The latter consist of a program in which you're a student half the time and are employed the other half in an occupation related to your field of study. A good deal of the training in technical fields consists of supplementary or extension courses for employed workers.

Types of Schools

In planning a program of training for a career in a technical field, you'll have to choose from among several types of institutions which offer this kind of training. The *private technical institutes* are either purely commercial enterprises or else are endowed, nonprofit schools. They usually limit their offerings to one of several restricted fields. In this way they can concentrate their efforts, provide extensive equipment, and develop successful placement opportunities in the industries for which they offer training. Some of these technical institutes cater mainly to local needs while others carry on extensive advertising and draw students from all parts of the country.

Public technical institutes are relatively few in number, being concentrated chiefly in New York State, Connecticut, Massachusetts, and California. These schools usually offer two-year programs in engineering and in a number of other fields including agriculture and seamanship.

A substantial number of *junior colleges* offer two-year programs in specific technical fields. Most of these schools are under public control, and tuition often is nominal. In many states and areas enrollments are restricted to residents of the state, county or city. Some of these colleges specialize to such an extent that they become recognized as vocational agricultural schools, technical institutes, and the like. . . .

Colleges and universities in increasing numbers are providing less than four-year programs of technical and other types of nonprofessional training. A number of them now have technical institutes and other types of vocational programs, most of which are of two years' duration. Many have extension programs in various communities, while others offer only on-campus courses during evenings and on Saturdays. Thirteen state schools and probably an equal number of privately endowed schools are known to offer such programs.

Admission Requirements

Practically all schools offering less than four-year technical programs require high school graduation or its equivalent as a basic admission requirement. Courses in mathematics and physics are required by many schools and by other courses.

Most publicly supported schools admit only residents of the state, county, or city, or give preference to applicants who have such residence qualifications. Several schools limit enrollment to those now employed in the field in which they seek further training, while a few others give preference to those with some job experience.

The endowed low-tuition schools have far more applicants than many of the proprietary schools and thus are more selective in their choice of students. Many judge the suitability of an applicant on the basis of an interview and his school record. Others select on the basis of the high school record and teachers' recommendations, while a few give aptitude tests in addition.

Schools that offer training in particularly popular subjects, such as electronics, are apt to be overcrowded, with several times as many applicants as can be accommodated.

Many schools simply maintain a waiting list of applicants who meet their basic requirements for admission, enrolling them according to date of application. If you're now in your third or fourth year in high school and have already decided upon a career in a technical field, you should lose no time in filing your application.

It's been estimated that women make up about 3 per cent of the total enrollment in the privately controlled schools. There are few or no restrictions on the enrollment of women students in technical schools or in technical programs offered by universities. It appears that relatively few women are interested in this field, hence the low enrollment percentage.

Types of Courses Offered

Technical schools offer training in over fifty different occupations, ranging from aircraft instruments mechanics to watchmaking. Many of the courses labeled "engineering" actually prepare the student for various subprofessional engineering positions rather than for professional work. The same is true of courses in ceramic technology and industrial chemistry. We list below some of the courses offered by the major technical schools.

Aeronautical

Aircraft construction and design
Aircraft maintenance engineering
Aircraft instrument technician
Airline maintenance engineering
Airplane drafting and detail design
Airport control
Aircraft instruments
Aviation communication
Aviation technology
Aviation and transportation

Architectural

Architectural drafting
Building construction
Building design
Construction industries
Architectural construction
Construction engineering

Chemical

Practical chemistry
Plastics
Industrial chemistry
Paint technology
Laboratory technology
Technical chemistry
Ceramics

Civil

Highway construction and surveying
Surveying and construction
Surveying
Cost estimating
Structural design
Public works engineering
Structural technology

Electrical

Electrical industries
Electrical machinery
Electrical theory and practice
Electrical machinery and power
Technical electricity
Broadcast operating
Industrial electrical engineering
Industrial electricity
Industrial electronics
Radio electronics engineering

Radio and communications
Electrical construction
Electro technician

Industrial

Tool engineering
Production techniques
Production management
Die design engineering
Production supervision
Testing and inspection
Time study

Mechanical

Heat power
Heat engineering
Refrigeration
Machine construction and tool design
Air conditioning
Essentials of mechanical engineering
Power generation
Mechanical design
Marine steam and diesel engineering
Heating and ventilating
Mechanical industries
Mechanical technology
Steam and diesel engineering
Machine design

Fuels and lubricants
Mechanical principles and practices
Tool design

Metallurgical and Mining

Industrial metallurgy
Heat treatment
Metallography
Welding technology
Oil technology
Petroleum engineering
Mining technology

Textile

Textile engineering
Textile chemistry and dyeing
Textile technology
Carding and spinning
Cotton manufacturing
Textile design
Synthetic textiles

Miscellaneous

Junior engineering
Sales and service engineering
Horology
Industrial design
Photographic technology
Drafting and design
Drafting and engineering

Length of Course

Courses offered by technical institutes may extend for only one year or as long as four, particularly if classes are arranged on a part-time basis. The total number of class hours also depends on the type of course and on the kind of institution offering the course. Some schools provide more intensive programs than others. You should bear in mind that a 1,000-class-hour course in airplane mechanics in one school may be better than or not as good as a 1,800-class-hour course in another school.

If you're interested in such a course you should obtain the catalogs of a number of schools and examine their offerings.

Usually you'll do well to steer clear of an unusually short course or one that is considerably longer than the average. If it's important that you become self-supporting at the earliest possible date, then you should look with favor on a more intensive course. You may find one school offering a course that extends over two years but which actually provides only 700 class hours. Another school will offer the same course in a period of six or eight months.

You should also weigh carefully the merits of a full-time course versus holding down a job and getting your training on a part-time basis. Most technical schools offer both part- and full-time training opportunities.

Some technical schools offer a "bachelor's degree" to students who complete their less than four-year training program. Such degrees however are substandard and aren't recognized by employers. The possessor of such a degree is likely to prejudice his case for employment by presenting a diploma of this type. Accredited technical schools offer only certificates of completion. Colleges and universities offering a full-time four-year course in engineering award a bachelor's degree to those who complete the course.

There are a few technical schools which, while not offering college degrees, make extravagant claims regarding their courses, such as "equal to or better than a college course." You should be wary of such claims, and investigate before investing in such a course. . . .

Placement Services

One of the advantages of attending a proprietary technical school is the fact that they usually have good placement services and are able to place nearly all their graduates. Nearby industries regularly send their scouts to the schools to interview the next crop of graduates and to make them offers of employment. These schools make every effort to maintain close ties with the industries for which they train workers so that they can do an effective placement job.

Other types of technical schools generally maintain adequate placement offices and are visited by representatives of industry seeking to line up new employees. The relationship with employers sometimes is not as close as in the case of proprietary schools and many graduates must depend on their own initiative to find jobs. The nonprofit schools don't feel that it's their obligation to place all of their graduates, though they try to aid as many as they can in landing jobs.

OTHER EDUCATIONAL RESOURCES[6]

Just where do you stand if you lack a college degree? Let's look at the facts: . . . The number of young people engaged in higher learning today [1957]—more than 3 million—may seem staggering.

But if statistics give you the idea just about everyone has gone to college, here's the other side of the coin:

More than 60 per cent of our population over twenty-five years of age have had an eighth-grade education or less.

Fourteen per cent have had less than five years of schooling.

Twenty-nine per cent have spent some time in high school, or graduated.

Only 11 per cent have gone to college, or beyond. . . . In terms of getting the kind of work you desire, the college degree is undoubtedly useful. But a college diploma is less important as far as jobs go than ability, imagination, and energy. In almost every occupation, the man or woman willing to start at the bottom of the ladder, and educate himself, will be watched carefully for promise and promotion.

The more basic differences between the college graduate and the man who didn't go to college can also be surmounted. . . . The things that really count—confidence, understanding and development of a broad-minded, dynamic attitude toward life—can be acquired off-campus, as well as on. . . . For the noncollege man and the college man alike . . . the key to learning lies in reading.

An organized reading program is of great value. Here your librarian can help you. No two persons need have the same

[6] From *So You Didn't Go To College*, pamphlet by Jerry Klein, associate editor of *Family Weekly*, and Bill Fisher, Jr., president of a public relations firm, Fisher, Dermer and Associates, Inc. (Public Affairs Pamphlet no 249) Public Affairs Committee. 22 E. 38th St. New York 16. '57. p 3-28. Reprinted by permission.

program, but there are certain essentials in a well-rounded plan. . . . [The great novels of all time] will not only provide hundreds of hours of fascinating reading, but will lay the basis for a greater understanding of the world we live in. Books like Wells's *Outline of History* will help open up the storehouse of knowledge of man's past. *Mathematics for the Millions* by Lancelot Hogben offers a basic understanding of mathematical science. And your reading can be further channeled into economics, government, literature, music, philosophy, science, and religion by helpful volumes like *Reading for Enjoyment* by Donald MacCampbell. . . .

For those who want more guidance in their reading, there is the "Great Books" program developed at the University of Chicago. This program involves reading selections from the classics and then discussing them. . . .

The [Great Books] Foundation has mapped a five-year reading program, each year's supply of paper-bound books costing about $11. Participants in the program read each book, then discuss it in groups which meet in such places as public libraries and community centers, with the help of a discussion leader who has completed a special course with the Foundation. . . .

A truly educated man will not limit himself to the study of the masterpieces of the past. He will also try to find out as much as he can about the world of today. This may require a little effort. It involves the careful reading of the more significant articles in a really good daily newspaper like the New York *Times,* the *Christian Science Monitor,* or Washington *Post and Times-Herald.* For mental stimulus a weekly magazine of opinion and a good monthly magazine should prove invaluable and give you the kind of information that will make you a more effective citizen. . . .

For millions of men and women all across the country, the answer both to vocational advancement and spiritual and intellectual broadening has started with spare-time courses in an endless variety of subjects, designed primarily to meet the needs of Americans who haven't gone to college. In a phrase—adult education. . . . There are courses in almost every vocational and technical subject imaginable and a wide choice of cultural subjects. The favorites include:

1. *Remedial.* Public speaking, diction, vocabulary building.
2. *Cultural.* Creative writing, music, art, literature, languages, psychology.
3. *Social.* Personality development, marriage and family, parenthood, dancing, hobbies, child care.
4. *Vocational Advancement.* Salesmanship, photography, cooking, sewing, interior decorating. . . .

Trade Union Education

Among the first organizations to recognize the value of adult education were the labor unions. In fact, one of the first adult education programs came in 1820 when the General Society of Mechanics and Tradesmen opened a library in New York City for "the general diffusion of light in every class of society."

Today education occupies a major place in trade unionism. Local classes, summer schools, short courses, full-year projects, weekend institutes, conferences—these are only a few of the instruments employed by labor. Some of these continue the early emphasis on "workers' education"—courses to provide knowledge which will help workers meet everyday labor-management situations, i.e., collective bargaining, shop stewardship, economics, history, parliamentary law.

But union leadership has been quick to sense members' need for more general education. The International Ladies' Garment Workers' Union was among the first to broaden the base of workers' education with courses in public speaking, science, music appreciation, and dramatics—all free.

One of its locals, the Dressmakers, established an art school some years ago, to provide opportunity for self-expression and relief from the monotony of machine jobs. Classes were held in the evenings, and the union provided both the instruction and the materials. . . .

Industry and Business

But if the unions have striven to broaden educational programs for their members, American business and industry have at least kept pace. . . .

By the hundreds of thousands, employees are going back to school, with the encouragement—often the blessing and sometimes the cash—of their employers.

Training Programs

Mill and Factory Magazine recently polled a sizable segment of American industry on its views regarding the use and value of training programs. Of the 31 per cent of companies maintaining training programs, 93 per cent found they helped offset the shortage of engineers and technicians; 68 per cent found employees eager to advance their education; 74 per cent thought company morale improved because of the plans; and 80 per cent thought the plans increased employee productivity.

The programs take various forms. Larger companies actually carry on classroom work within the plant, usually in the evening. Others use facilities of local public schools or universities, usually picking up all or part of the worker's tuition tab. Thousands of firms have arrangements with correspondence schools for employee home-study courses.

Nor are all industry plans designed to help the worker increase his on-the-job productivity only. Many encompass courses unrelated to the worker's job, but designed to make him a healthier, happier, better-informed human being.

At Western Electric's Cicero, Illinois, plant, for example, a company school gives so-called "fundamental" and leisure-time courses in addition to many vocational subjects. For about $3.50 per thirteen-week course, an employee can learn algebra and trigonometry, English, industrial statistics, electricity and electronics, public speaking. Leisure-time courses include sketching and painting, piano lessons, gym, and photography. In the vocational division, there's blueprint reading, mechanical drawing, assembly and detail drawing, metallurgy of iron and steel, milling machine operation, and dial system telephony.

At International Harvester, Chicago, there are in-plant courses in such subjects as personal qualities of a foreman, public speaking, and economics.

Johns-Manville has a company-wide program to reimburse 65 per cent of tuition, fees, and transportation for completed courses in schools and colleges. At Standard Oil, the Esso

Educational Refund Plan provides reimbursement for a major portion of a student's tuition for courses which bear on his present job, or one he might be assigned to in the near future.

Many industries in the Chicago area finance their employees' education at the Illinois Institute of Technology, and the Institute in turn offers extension courses especially designed to meet the needs of individual companies.

At Eastman Kodak, close to two thousand employees are taking advantage of a tuition-aid program for job-related college-level courses. Southwestern Bell Telephone Company has enrolled about fourteen hundred in undergraduate and graduate studies under its plan, and Convair, largest division of General Dynamics, underwrites college extension courses in two cities in cooperation with the University of California at Los Angeles. . . .

Home-Study Courses

Probably the fastest-growing tool for employee training for industry today is home study. In fact, close to five thousand business and industrial organizations have initiated cooperative training arrangements with a single home-study school alone, International Correspondence Schools of Scranton, Pennsylvania. Their list includes many of the nation's leading companies—seven of the top firms, and seventy-two of the first hundred in rank. . . .

Home study has changed—and improved radically over the years.

Its greatest impetus came during the depression, when more than $7 million was poured into correspondence schools in tuition, and more than eighty colleges and universities established their own home-study programs.

World War II brought another boost. By July 1946, more than a million servicemen and women, many in combat areas, had registered for correspondence courses through the United States Armed Forces Institute. They received millions of self-teaching texts and thousands of language records in scores of tongues.

The effect was lasting. Today, more than 2 million persons throughout the world are engaged in correspondence school studies. In the United States alone, nearly 150 colleges and universities enroll 175,000 students annually in home-study work; the USAFI, nearly 250,000; the Marine Corps Institute, 22,000; and the nation's 450 private correspondence schools, close to 750,000—more than the total number of freshmen enrolled in all U.S. colleges and universities.

The typical home-study "undergrad," it is reported, is twenty-six or twenty-seven, married, has one child, and is employed full-time as a manual or semiskilled worker. In the 1890's, the average student had only a few grades of schooling. By 1915, he had completed eight grades. Today, he is a high school graduate.

Students—and they range from teen-agers to great-grand-mothers—pay $25 to $500 a course, and devote an average of ten hours a week to study. How quickly a student completes a course depends on the course itself, and how fast he progresses.

In today's correspondence schools you can learn anything from aeronautics or atomic energy to highway engineering, from navigation to personnel and labor relations, from plastics to pulp and paper-making, from accounting to short story writing. Courses in nonvocational subjects like homemaking, sewing, and art still attract sizable enrollments, but, for the most part, the heavy emphasis is on job-related instruction. A list of one school's most popular courses includes: mechanical, electrical, and civil engineering; mechanical drafting, radio and TV servicing, accounting, electronics, math, architecture, industrial foremanship, and tool design. . . .

Agricultural Extension Service

Correspondence education has always had great appeal in rural areas, where there was often no other opportunity for adult education. The leader in this field is the Agricultural Extension Service operated by the various land-grant universities.

Together with the state colleges of agriculture, the Extension Service is the largest single tax-supported adult education institution in the world. Founded in 1914, its staff numbers more than 10,000. The vast majority are county agents and home demonstration agents who teach or plan a wide variety of vocational, cultural, and leisure-time subjects. Their services, available in most of the counties in the United States, are paid for by county, state, and Federal Government.

At one time the Service's rural teaching emphasized vocational farm subjects—marketing, animal husbandry, dairying, poultry, housing, rural community organization, sanitation, care of farm equipment. Today, in addition to these staples, rural men and women can learn about clothing, canning, recreation, home food processing, home decoration, household budgeting, and child care. Beyond this, more than 100,000 farm men belong to clubs organized to discuss public questions—with federally supplied discussion materials.

Drama, music, and art are also occupying an increasingly important part in the rural training program. In one state alone, sixteen thousand have taken the Extension Service's music courses. Reading programs, many supplied through "bookmobiles"—libraries on wheels—are growing in popularity. Once a year, the Extension Service sponsors a music festival in which more than fifteen hundred rural music groups participate.

University Extension Services

The growth of these programs, of course, is a reflection of the general expansion of university extension work since the war—though extension programs have been operating in U.S. colleges and universities since the early nineteenth century.

Extension means many things—correspondence courses, lectures, summer schools, press and publications services, evening schools, lending libraries, film and visual aid programs, conferences, institutes, broadcasting services, and short courses. And this varied fare is designed primarily for adult students who work during the day. Many courses do not carry college credits, but it is possible to earn academic credits in evening and Saturday courses and qualify for training in nursing, teaching, and other professions.

The state agricultural colleges play a leading role in the rural education program for adults. At Kansas State College, for example, night courses include soil management and crop rotation; animal, dairy, and poultry husbandry; farm management; marketing; home health and sanitation; land use planning; recreation.

Probably more than any other single medium of organized adult education, extension facilities are *used.* By and large, they attract adult audiences—92 per cent are over twenty years of age—anxious for new knowledge either for job betterment, or for greater understanding. . . .

Since most students sandwich their educational pursuits between full-time employment and family life, extension educators have established dozens of practical job-related courses, most at relatively nominal fees. The Technical Extension Division of Purdue University, for example, trains engineering aides specifically to support the work of graduate, professional engineers. Its courses in basic knowledge and practices of present-day industry emphasize the applied, rather than the theoretical.

Another important "plus" for university extension is that it often takes the college to the people. It conducts traveling schools, like one established by the University of Washington, where a special corps of faculty members makes one to three appearances daily before groups of all kinds in about 130 cities in the state. Many schools, like Indiana University, have established centers in cities throughout their state. Indiana has branches in eight other communities, and also offers more than four hundred correspondence courses.

The six units of the City College of New York are typical of the broad range of subject matter available to adults through extension services. Included in the catalog of several hundred evening courses are: anthropology, building construction, camp counseloring, cosmetics, crocheting, Danish, engineering, homemaking, Icelandic, literature, music, parent-child [relations], personality development, public relations, sports, stamp collecting, television, window display.

The same institution has proved its worth as an innovator. It established courses especially for housewives reluctant to leave their offspring alone while they go to school. Now mother and child pursue together the mysteries of arts and crafts, foreign languages, recorder playing, piano, and folk dancing.

City College also serves as a built-in baby-sitter. While mother goes along to her classes, youngsters in the seven-to-twelve age group are dropped off in a special arts and crafts class. Knowing that junior is being kept constructively out of mischief, mom is able to attend her eight-week class in, say, "Dog Care," which, according to the City College catalog, is "a practical course for all who own or love dogs."...

The Brooklyn College . . . [Special Baccalaureate Degree Program for Adults] attempts to translate the life experiences of students into conventional college credits, instead of requiring adult men and women to take college courses in subjects they've already learned through practical experience. Interviews and tests determine the extent of a student's knowledge in a given area. Then he makes up only his deficiencies through regular classroom work....

YM-YW Programs

Many YMCA's provide opportunities for persons to acquire skills, to grow in self-understanding, to enjoy hobbies, and to take responsible leadership in community life. One YMCA is currently offering ninety informal education courses. Included in the offerings of YMCA's are opportunities for vocational improvement such as: dictation for medical secretaries, human relations in the office, effective letter writing, rapid reading and comprehension, advanced stenography, and persuasive selling. Public affairs interests are explored in YMCA informal education groups. Forums on "How to Improve Our Community" and "Issues Confronting the Nation" are popular.

Courses available at YWCA's vary from community to community. They may run the gamut from classes for acquiring skills in sports like swimming, tennis, skiing, and sail boating to a program of scientific weight control or education for childbirth. Brush-up courses can be taken in typing, shorthand, or languages. One can join in appreciation of good music, art, and literature; or take part in a chorus, paint a picture, or act in a play. Some of these opportunities are available to men as well as women, and often to the entire family. If a YWCA doesn't have a particular course that a number of people want, it can be started!

Other Possibilities

Among groups which have consistently pursued new knowledge through organized reading programs are the voluntary associations —women's clubs, settlement houses, church groups. Sometimes these programs take the form of weekly or monthly book "reviews" delivered orally by one of the members of the group.

But in groups of this kind, which often operate on the principle of education coupled with social action, reading is only one source of learning. Many women's clubs sponsor lecture series. Luncheon clubs like Lions, Rotary, and Kiwanis often peg lecture subjects to current community-betterment projects. So do PTA's and groups like the League of Women Voters.

In Evanston, Illinois, the League sponsors a nine-month program of lectures and discussion groups on local and foreign affairs, social welfare, education and economics. Members put knowledge to use in community projects.

Parent-teacher groups also carry on year-round educational programs. The National Congress of Parents and Teachers provides course materials to thousands of member organizations. In Oak Park, Illinois, the PTA offers courses like "Life Is What You Make It" and "How to Handle Money."

Church groups, accessible to all, have often been leaders in community adult education. The Oakton United Church, Evanston, Illinois, for example, conducts adult courses like "Building a Mature Philosophy of Sex" and "Family Budgeting of Money and Leisure Time." Added to these are square dancing, a women's guild, lectures, forums, panel discussions, and debates on current affairs. . . .

Although located principally in larger cities, settlement houses have enhanced the lives of millions of men and women through sound educational programs. . . .

The range of subject matter in many settlement houses is fantastic: parliamentary procedure, discussion leadership, civics, homemaking, art and music, public housing, politics, public affairs, health education, consumer education, parent education.

Drama and theatre groups have long been favorites. Since World War II home planning and do-it-yourself workshops have appeared. There are special programs for "senior citizens," others for youngsters and teen-agers.

Often, settlement house groups form community councils to improve local conditions such as traffic hazards, housing, lack of play space, or smoke control, and are active in fostering better race relations. In one settlement, a group of adult clubs of different nationalities and races devised a project to develop appreciation of the contributions of Negroes to American life. The result was an exhibit which traveled to public schools and libraries all over the United States.

The Henry Street Settlement [in New York City], one of the most famous institutions of its kind in the world, publishes its own newspaper and operates a credit union, besides conducting many adult courses including a home-planning workshop in furniture making and repair, sewing and shoe mending.

The People's Guild of Brooklyn, New York, found that mothers and homemakers rarely had evenings free to attend courses. It inaugurated group reading circles where serious books could be discussed during afternoon sessions in members' homes.

The same is true of the growing number of programs operated by the school authorities of our cities. For it is here that the "school-around-the-clock" idea is finding particularly dramatic expression.

Youngsters attend city schools by day. After dusk, they are opened to millions of young adults and older men and women. In New York City alone, 38,947 adults work by day and in the evening attend more than one hundred elementary schools spotted throughout the city's five boroughs. More than 25,000 others participate in "informal" evening programs featuring dance, handicrafts, sports, music, cooking and other spare-time skills. Thousands of others use city facilities to learn new trades or improve their mastery of daytime jobs.

Though it is the largest city in the country, New York's program is not unusual. In Des Moines, Iowa, you can learn acetylene welding, architecture, and radio repair at night. The Baltimore evening program will teach you income tax and insurance, English, and citizenship. A discussion series for mothers of adolescents is just one of many offerings in Jackson, Michigan. If you live in Stamford, Connecticut, there's "Good Grooming for Women," in addition to many more conventional courses.

In San Jose, California, where more than one out of every six adults are registered, the city offers more than one hundred courses. Birmingham, Alabama, has established ten recreation centers where parents and children often attend the same courses. Los Angeles has a Bureau of Music which organizes singing groups in more than twenty-five communities within the city.

Sac City, Iowa, established an advisory council on adult education back in 1931. Forty citizens, male and female, representing town and farm interests, meet regularly with the local school superintendent and the vocational, agriculture, and homemaking teachers. Together, they plan courses in home equipment, industrial arts, copper work, child development, salesmanship, current events, photography, swimming, typing, driver training.

Toward a Richer Life

It is particularly interesting to find more and more people seeking inner growth and self-development without necessarily thinking of any material benefit that may result. With the financial assistance of the Fund for Adult Education, a number of cities have set up groups to discuss world affairs, public issues, economics, and the humanities.

The Cleveland Public Library has sponsored for some years now a series of discussion programs under the general title of "Invitation to Ideas." The American Foundation for Political Education and the Foreign Policy Association in cooperation with local libraries and councils on world affairs have conducted discussion groups in more than one hundred cities on world politics based on some of the world's greatest political writings. . . .

On every level, adult education programs are becoming broader, deeper, and more significant each day. But, like everything else, adult education, to be truly useful, must be *used*.

HIGH SCHOOL DROPOUTS [7]

The high school dropout has long been a source of concern. Even today, despite the strides that have been made in developing a school program designed to retain all youth through the completion of their secondary education, too many are leaving school before they graduate. [Abraham A. Ribicoff, Secretary of Health, Education and Welfare, anticipated in October 1961 that 2.5 million of the 10.8 million students enrolled in grades

[7] From pamphlet published by the Department of Classroom Teachers and Research Division, National Education Association. 1201 16th St. N.W. Washington 6, D.C. '59. p 1-20. Reprinted by permission.

nine through twelve of the nation's public and nonpublic schools will drop out before graduation—Ed.]

Today's dropouts will continue to present a problem long into the future. . . . How meaningful a contribution can [they] be expected to make to the economic, social, and political life of the community, without having had the advantages offered by those understandings which the school proposes to give to all youth? . . .

Compulsory school attendance laws alone cannot hold the youth, since the real problem is not the number of years he spends in school. Studies have shown that the average dropout stays in school almost as long as graduates do, but because he is usually retained in one or more grades, he has not, at the end of his compulsory school stay, had the full benefit of a high school education. It is the acquisition of such a complete secondary school education that is the vital point. While it is recognized that the traditional high school program cannot answer the needs of all types of pupils, some program could be devised to take care of most of them.

The youth himself will find more and more frequently that occupational opportunities are severely restricted for anyone not holding a high school diploma. . . . [See "Job Outlook for Young Job-Hunters" and "The Plight of the Unskilled," in Section II, below.]

As a matter of fact, the U.S. Department of Labor recently reported that seventy-one occupations currently affected by a shortage of personnel required a minimum education of four years of high school. And its *Job Guide for Young Workers*, which listed eighty-five jobs frequently available to young people of high school age, mentioned only twenty-three which did not require a high school diploma. . . .

On the average, a high school graduate's earnings during his adult years will exceed those of a high school dropout by $30,000, and they will be $50,000 greater than those of a person who has gone no farther than the eighth grade. These estimates are based on 1950 Census data. Every indication is that the differences would be even more pronounced on the basis of today's wage and salary scales. . . .

As the possession of a high school diploma becomes more nearly universal, failure to have one will lead in many cases to feelings of inferiority, further complicated by the rejections encountered in job opportunities. In the long run, these maladjustments may result in antisocial behavior. *It has been shown that the incidence of delinquency is 10 times higher among dropouts than among high school graduates.* . . .

According to statistics published by the United States Office of Education, the high school graduating class of 1954 contained only 553 of the 1,000 pupils who had been enrolled in the fifth grade seven years earlier. Similarly, the same class of 1954 contained only 634 . . . of the 1,000 members of the ninth grade four years earlier. . . . The first major drop occurs between the ninth grade and the tenth grade, when many pupils are making the transition between junior and senior high school. . . . Another significant drop occurs between the tenth and eleventh grades. Many of these pupils have obviously tried the secondary school and found it wanting for their needs. . . . It has . . . been found that pupils who drop out from the eighth, ninth, and tenth grades most often do so for reasons closely related to their school experiences, such as grade retardation, academic difficulties, and failure to participate in pupil activities. Dropouts from the later grades, however, are chiefly accounted for by other well-defined reasons such as marriage or the need to work.

Statistics can help give us an idea of the type of individual most likely to become a dropout. Most surprising and significant is the fact that it is not necessarily the less intelligent who leave school before graduation. . . . However, it is true that many dropouts have histories of poor achievement in school. The discouragement which accompanies academic failure leads to disinterest in school and eagerness to enter the world of adult concerns.

Most youths who drop out do so at the age of sixteen . . . [when] most of them would be starting their junior year in high school. The time immediately following a vacation is a particularly hazardous one since the impulse not to return to the school routine is strong.

The typical dropout is also frequently characterized by failure to belong to an in-school group. He usually does not participate in extracurricular activities, which constitute an area of interest and identification for many students. His relationships with his teachers are poor; and depending upon the community and community values as to education, his relationships with his fellow students may also be tense and strained.

Frequently the dropout has a poor attendance record as well as a history of resistance to school authority. As a result of his academic disinterest and failure, the average dropout is retarded by at least two years.

To compound all these difficulties, he encounters attitudes at home which serve only to reinforce his own. His parents often place little value on education and school achievement. And quite apart from the pressures of real financial need, he frequently meets at home an atmosphere of impatience with the amount of time he is spending at school rather than in a wage-earning job. . . .

The reason most often given by students for leaving school upon reaching the statutory age is the necessity to secure remunerative employment. Statistics vary widely in this connection. In one study, 39 per cent reported quitting school because they wanted to go to work, and 21 per cent stated that the family needed financial help. In another study, 69 per cent gave as their reason the fact that money was badly needed.

Certainly this is a cogent argument. Older children in large families frequently are faced with the grim necessity of helping to support the rest of the family. . . .

However, in many instances where financial need is cited, it is not the real reason why a young person leaves school. A boy or girl who dislikes school and feels that working would be preferable may cite the desire for employment as his reason for dropping out when actually no financial need exists.

Even where the youth sincerely feels the urgent need of money, his definition of need may well be questioned. It is sometimes merely the need to support a car. In other cases, however, not only is money needed at home, but the very expenses connected with the youth's school attendance place an intolerable burden upon the family. . . .

Perhaps the most crucial influence exerted by the home is in the area of attitude. The feelings of the parents toward school, especially those of the mother, play an important role in shaping the attitudes of the child. If throughout his early years he can see that his parents value the opportunity to acquire an education, even though they themselves may not have much formal schooling, and if he knows that they place a high value on his performance at school, he usually can be expected to take a positive attitude toward the school. If parents consistently support, in their relations with their child, the actions of the teachers, the child will transfer to the teacher some of the respect he feels for his parents.

On the other hand, parents who are extremely demanding of their children in terms of scholastic performance may merely add to their feelings of inadequacy and discouragement. Each child needs to find at home a positive attitude toward the educational advantages which are being offered him, together with sincere encouragement for him to do his best. This is by no means the same thing as undue pressure.

Closely related to home values are the values the child senses in the community. It is not unusual, in fact, for a child to be influenced more by the values and attitudes of his peers or of members of the community whom he respects than by his parents. If the community grants more importance to high immediate earnings than to the long-range benefits of education, or if such earnings are needed to help the student keep up with what others are doing, it becomes exceedingly difficult for the student to adopt an attitude at variance with this. . . .

It cannot be denied that if a pupil felt the school was giving him something useful, he would not be inclined to leave before graduating. Pupils leave because they are not interested in what they are doing, because they see no connection between school work and life, and because they feel they could use their time more constructively in other ways. The immediate job of the schools, then, is to show them that they are wrong. Young people must be made to see the value of what they are doing and experiencing.

For most dropouts the crux of the problem is the inadequacy of the curriculum. They find in the old traditional curriculum little which appears to relate to their needs and interests. They are not convinced of the relationships between the work of the class and the realities of everyday life.

Teachers can help overcome this obstacle by stressing the vocational values inherent in the subjects which they are teaching, for every subject being taught has such values. . . .

To the potential dropout, being able to apply his school experience to everyday living is a meaningful inducement for completing the school program.

One step in the right direction is the widely diversified curriculum. In such a setup, the subject offerings may be expected to appeal to a wide segment of the youth.

Naturally the prerequisite for such a curriculum is a thorough grounding in the fundamentals. Without this, no one can achieve his full potential, either in his school years or in his later life. Therefore, the teaching of the three R's to each individual pupil must remain a basic function of the schools.

In addition to this basic program, the schools should provide other courses which meet more specialized needs. By offering elective courses in the various interest areas of students, a school achieves two purposes: it encourages the pupil to remain in school, and it equips him with a really salable asset and renders him ready to enter the world of employment upon graduation. One school which sends few of its students to college has inaugurated courses in such diverse areas as barbering, shoe repair, commercial cooking, auto-body repair, and the like, so as to help every pupil in the school reach a worthy goal. . . .

Not only must the scope of the subjects offered be widened so as to appeal to all pupils, but some attention must be given to adjusting the content levels of the offerings in such a way that every pupil can find something for himself. . . . In schools in which efforts have been concentrated in this direction, the significance of the IQ has diminished in distinguishing between dropouts and those who stay. This indicates that even those with low IQ's are finding useful things in the school program, and so they do not feel the impulse to leave. . . .

The role of guidance in holding the potential dropout in school is a vital one. . . . In one school, the drop-out rate fell from 45 per cent to 26 per cent between 1943 and 1954. This result was largely attributed to a comprehensive guidance program aimed at drawing youths into the curriculum for which they were particularly suited and at making the most of their own natural interests and abilities.

Some schools have found that orientation classes help meet the needs of the potential dropout, in that they enable him to learn, in a pleasant way, what the school has to offer to him as an individual and to all young people as they prepare to take their place in the world. . . .

Some schools have experimented with plans in which a few pupils were assigned to individual teachers, who were then to take a particular interest in them and their problems. As a result, these pupils came to feel that at least one teacher was especially interested in them, and accordingly, this personal relationship which developed out of such intensive work resulted in improved education and adjustment. This is another expression of the need of the pupil to feel that he "belongs.". . .

There are still many instances in which youths are obliged to quit school because of financial reasons. In some cases, their earning power is necessary to the family. In others, the costs of attending school are prohibitive.

This problem has been solved in some schools through cooperative work plans, by which the youth engages in supervised work under the direction of the school and for which he receives credit.

II. EMPLOYMENT

EDITOR'S INTRODUCTION

Because there are many easily accessible sources of information on a variety of occupations, this section makes no attempt to supply data on specific careers (except military service). Instead it presents some employment trends which will affect the young worker of the 1960's.

The first article, from *Editorial Research Reports,* predicts that "the young job-hunter is going to have an increasingly harder time finding stable employment than did his older brother" because of increased competition from his contemporaries and rising demands for training and education.

Jerome M. Rosow, of the Standard Oil Company (New Jersey), explains next why the unskilled worker in particular is at a disadvantage in a "society of specialization," while in the third selection, Charles C. Killingsworth, professor of labor and industrial relations at Michigan State University, examines the meaning of automation and its effects on employment in industry.

President Kennedy drew attention to the serious nature of youth employment problems when he created, in November 1961, a special committee of Federal, state and local representatives to encourage the development of work opportunities for youth. Nearly one million people between the ages of sixteen and twenty-one were unemployed—neither at school nor at work—in 1961. Another new body established by the President is the President's Committee on Equal Employment Opportunity, which is empowered to enforce nondiscriminatory hiring policies by contractors working on government projects. Negroes and other nonwhites have long undergone the devitalizing experience of seeing their training wasted in menial jobs as a result of racial discrimination by employers. "American Negroes—A Wasted Resource" surveys the Negro employment picture and the effect of discrimination on industry.

The fifth selection, from the pamphlet *You and Your Career*, outlines the general occupational categories in the world of work and suggests some evaluations the student should make as he considers his choice of career. "Military Service as a Career" gives some facts of particular interest to young men who must meet their selective service obligations.

OUTLOOK FOR YOUNG JOB-HUNTERS [1]

American youths entering the job market during the 1940's and early 1950's had a relatively easy time finding work. The great economic expansion of the war and postwar years provided ample employment opportunities except in brief periods of recession. Competition for jobs was reduced by manpower demands of the military services and by opening of educational opportunities to veterans under the GI bills.

Increasing Competition in the Search for Jobs

The situation is now changing and is likely to change still more in the near future. The GI education program has tapered off and the number of enlisted personnel in the armed forces has fallen from about 3 million in 1953, when the Korean War ended, to around 2 million today. Of greater significance are the impending growth of the population in the school-leaving ages and a decline in job opportunities for untrained and inexperienced workers. All these factors make it certain that the young job-hunter is going to have an increasingly harder time finding stable employment than did his older brother.

Secretary of Labor Arthur J. Goldberg told this year's college graduates, in an open letter on May 28 [1961], that their prospects for employment were good despite a persisting high rate of unemployment. A less happy job prospect faces young people without a college education. Surveys made by state employment agencies in fifteen industrial areas last April, before business had picked up so noticeably, showed that the effects of employment cutbacks in industry were particularly severe on young job-hunters, especially those who had not completed a

[1] From "Jobs for Young People," by Helen B. Shaffer, staff writer for *Editorial Research Reports*. *Editorial Research Reports*. 11:501-6. Jl. 12, '61. Reprinted by permission.

high school education. With an ample supply of applicants for job openings, employers favored experienced older workers over inexperienced youths.

Pittsburgh reported that jobs normally filled by youths were being taken by married women reentering the labor market because their husbands were out of work. The Baltimore, Chicago, and New York surveys indicated that "automation and other technological changes in industry are gradually curtailing various traditional beginner jobs for young workers." One of Boston's largest public employment offices reported that applicants under twenty years of age constituted 22 per cent of the job-seekers but only 6 per cent of placements during the previous year.

It was brought out in the employment agency reports that existence of a substantial labor surplus had influenced employers to tighten skill and education requirements. A high school diploma was generally required and more and more employers expected applicants to have some college or other post-high school education. Some employers, not wanting to bother with work permits or compliance with other child labor law requirements, refused to consider any applicant under eighteen. A number of area reports, directing attention to the expected increase in the number of high school graduates, stressed that it would "intensify the already serious problem of absorbing young job-seekers into the labor market."

Unemployment among young workers has consistently run, in good times and bad, at no less than twice the rate for all workers. In May 1961, for example, the national unemployment rate was 6.7 per cent, but for workers aged sixteen to twenty the rate was 17 per cent.

Sharp Rise in Number of Job Market Entrants

The bulk of entrants into the labor force during the 1960's will be young people born in the postwar years of high birth rates. Twenty-six million persons under age twenty-five are expected to enter the labor force during the decade as against 19 million during the 1950's. The number of persons in the labor force still under twenty-five at the end of the 1950's was only half a million more than it had been at the beginning of the decade, having risen from 13.3 million to 13.8 million. But by 1970 the number of workers in this age bracket is expected to be 6.4 million greater than in 1960, rising by nearly 50 per cent to a total of 20.2 million.

By 1970 the proportion of the labor force comprising workers in the teens and early twenties will approach the figure recorded in the period before child labor and compulsory school attendance laws had been widely enacted. At the turn of the century 27 per cent of the male labor force had not reached the age of twenty-five. By 1955 the ratio had dropped to 17 per cent, but by 1970 it will have moved back to 23 per cent, a level at which it is expected to remain for at least five years.

Women in the labor force have had a different history. Nearly 50 per cent of all female workers in 1900 were under twenty-five, chiefly because most women did not work after they married. With an increasing number of older women holding jobs, the proportion under twenty-five had fallen to 20 per cent by 1960. In another ten years, however, the proportion of young women workers is expected to have risen to 24 per cent, where it will be almost the same as that of male workers under twenty-five. These figures have been said to "make it abundantly clear how dependent the American economy will be in the next decade or more upon the labor force participation, the skill and the productivity of the nation's young people."

Effect of Occupational Shifts on Job Openings

Labor Secretary Goldberg testified before a Senate Labor subcommittee, June 3, that "to appreciate the potential problem posed by this massive influx of young workers, it must be considered in light of the unemployment rate among our young people, as well as the changing character of the economy." He pointed to the following changes in the "occupational structure" which make it imperative that new members of the labor force have a solid background of general education plus training in certain specialties: the shift from an agricultural to an industrial and commercial economy, the rapid expansion of research and development, the application of technological improvements, the increasing size and complexity of business organizations, the growth of record-keeping, and the growing need for educational and medical services.

Opportunities for work on farms or in unskilled industrial jobs—areas in which one fifth of all workers under twenty-five were employed in 1957—are declining. The Labor Department expects also that jobs for factory operatives and other semi-skilled workers, which offered substantial employment opportunities to youth in the past, will expand at a declining rate. Greatest expansion will be in the professional, managerial and skilled occupations in which the percentage of workers under twenty-five has never been large. There will be a substantial growth of openings also for young clerical and sales workers, but educational and special training requirements in these fields are rising.

Although the educational attainments of youth as a whole are increasing, a substantial number of young people have glaring educational deficiencies: one in three of those who enroll in high school fails to graduate. An estimated 7.5 million teen-agers will enter the labor market during the 1960's without having completed high school; 2.5 million of them will not have completed the eighth grade. The nongraduates, said Goldberg, will face "a grave problem in finding useful employment in the years ahead."

Experience of School Dropouts in Labor Market

Virtually all youngsters who drop out of school, with the exception of girls who quit to marry, start looking for work. A number of studies offer statistical evidence of the handicaps under which they labor. The dropouts find it hardest to get work, they get the poorest jobs, they are laid off more frequently, their periods of unemployment last longer, and they make the least progress up the job scale as they reach the peak earning years of life. One study showed that more than one half of high school graduates, but only two fifths of the dropouts, found jobs in less than a week. Ten per cent of the dropouts, but only 4 per cent of the graduates, took as long as fourteen or more weeks to find the first job.

When job opportunities are curtailed, the dropout feels the pinch more than the high school graduate. The state employment agency surveys last April showed an "appreciably more difficult labor market situation faced by dropouts, as compared to high school graduates." Philadelphia, for example, reported that the decline in number of placements between the five-month period ended in February 1961 and the like period a year earlier was 50 per cent among dropouts as against only 6 per cent among high school graduates.

Comparison of occupational ratios among 1960 high school graduates and that year's dropouts showed that the better educated got more of the white-collar and skilled jobs, while the dropouts filled the poorer-paying jobs with the least prospect for continuous employment. Studies of older workers indicated that occupational differences related to educational background tended to persist throughout life.

THE PLIGHT OF THE UNSKILLED [2]

"Unskilled" is a negative word. Applied to the young worker in our society, it is a symbol of discouragement. In this solar age, man's knowledge is rushing headlong in new directions and creating greater demands for skill and education in the labor force. The undereducated and the undertrained young people who must struggle with the barest preparation are ill equipped to meet the future.

The future for unskilled people is contained within a triangle. This triangle is like a three-sided wall that cannot be scaled. On the one side, the unskilled worker is labeled as vulnerable. On the second side, he is marked as a static force in a very dynamic society. And, on the third side, he is listed as dispensable—among the most expendable of all workers. . . .

What is the deepest and most painful wound a worker can suffer? Certainly the loss of his job is the most severe injury. Time and again, the unemployment figures are populated by unskilled workers.

During the 1958 business decline, one half of the unemployed were in unskilled or semiskilled occupations. Almost 2.5 million workers with limited skill were thrown out of work. They were the first to go and the last to find new jobs. Unemployment

[2] From "Investment in the Future," article by Jerome M. Rosow, coordinator of industrial relations and classified compensation functions, Standard Oil Company (New Jersey). *American Child.* 42:5-8. Mr. '60. Reprinted by permission of the National Committee on Employment of Youth, division of the National Child Labor Committee, 419 Park Ave. S. New York 16.

doubled and tripled among these groups of our industrial society, when clerical and professional employees were almost fully employed.

The short recessions are mild and simple things against the background of America's great depression of the 1930's. But these recessions are not so mild for the unskilled, who feel every little bump in the business cycle. Once the unskilled lose their jobs, they cannot relocate quickly, and they remain out of work for long stretches of time. In the last recession, over half of all those unemployed twenty-seven weeks or longer were workers with limited skills. Skill, training, and education are real armor for industrial life today. Without them, the worker is really defenseless and vulnerable.

Major changes in manufacturing techniques produce profound effects upon the structure of skills and occupations. "Automation" is the big word of tomorrow. It simply means more mechanization—machines instead of men. In past decades, machines created more jobs for operatives (for men and women to tend the machines). Recent and future changes mean great gains in production without an equal rate of increase in semiskilled jobs. From 1910 to the present, the semiskilled work force increased faster than the labor force. However, in the next twenty years, the semiskilled occupations will grow at a slower rate than the nation's labor force. . . .

At the same time, professional and technical workers are needed to meet the industrial changes. Engineers, scientists, draftsmen, and technicians are increasing two and a half times as fast as the labor force as a whole. The elite of the machine age is and will be the highly educated experts.

Automation reduces monotony, machine pacing, and the heavy physical demand of jobs. Mass production jobs are safer and more pleasant. The new machine age will not hurt the unskilled worker. But it will force him to move around more to find work and to keep up with technological shifts. It will make him more machine-dependent than ever before. This is what it means to be static: unchanging in the face of a dynamic society.

Why is the unskilled worker dispensable?

1. Companies have a very low investment in training such workers and are quite ready to lose them.

2. The semiskilled are easily replaced from the general labor force, particularly during periods of some unemployment.

3. These workers are easily and quickly trained for the simple jobs. Many operations permit training on the production line in a few days.

4. The unskilled are very mobile. They change jobs quite often; several times a year is not unusual. In tight labor markets, where workers are scarce, the unskilled are the first to quit. They seek new jobs partly out of boredom and the dead-end nature of their jobs, partly out of the desire for more pay. During layoffs, they are the first hit. Although the unskilled are in motion, the movement is a closed circle: from job to job with little or no advancement. They scurry from one dead end to the next, searching for a road to progress and advancement. But the road is only open to those with skill, education, and training.

5. Low seniority is a factor in the high mobility. Since the semiskilled are in motion, they fail to build up the service credits that mean on-the-job seniority, which means job security. Furthermore, many seniority clauses in union contracts have occupational groupings that put the unskilled and semiskilled workers in competition among themselves. In addition, the higher skilled workers are permitted to claim jobs held by their juniors at lower skill levels when their own work is suspended or abolished. All this means that the low skill, low seniority worker is the first to go.

The prospects for the young worker with limited skill are not black and foreboding; they are gray and quite colorless and will always contain problems. The odds are heavily stacked against those individuals who are most plentiful in an industrial society. Workers who are deprived, or who deprive themselves, of the opportunity to elevate themselves above the lowest levels are helpless to accept the problems faced by the lowest levels.

The unskilled young worker is highly vulnerable to changes of both an economic and a technological nature. . . . The growing handicap of remaining without any special skill in a society of specialization should impress upon young people the necessity for more education and more training. In the main, a sense of devotion to an investment in themselves for their own future security is the basic issue.

EFFECTS OF AUTOMATION ON EMPLOYMENT [3]

What Is Automation?

The term, "automation," is only a little more than ten years old. During the time that it has been in use, it has seemed to be a word in search of a meaning. Some people have used it to cover almost all kinds of technological change. Others have applied it to one limited kind of technique, such as the mechanical transfer of parts from one operation to another. I believe that any useful definition of the term must be broad enough to identify the basic concepts involved, and limited enough to distinguish it from mechanization in general. My own definition is as follows: "Automation is the mechanization of thought, sensory, and control processes." This definition is intended to reflect the fact that scientists have recently developed a new theoretical framework concerning communication, control, and even thought. The definition also reflects the fact that automation is merely one aspect of mechanization, though a profoundly significant one. . . .

Perhaps the best known examples of automation are the giant "transfer machines" of the automobile manufacturers, which are about a block long [and] which can perform scores of operations on a part such as an engine block without human assistance (except for occasional tool changes or repairs). Actually, however, the transfer machines represent a rather elementary, perhaps even crude type of automation. Electronic computers are a more significant development. There is now an oil refinery in Texas which is completely controlled by a giant computer—and it does a much better job than the former human operators. Two computer-controlled chemical plants are now being built. Computers are revolutionizing the bookkeeping end of banking. They are making great strides in the field of inventory control. More and more of the processing of policies and claims in the insurance business is being handled by computers. The Air Force has . . . announced that it has a computer which is the key component of a machine that translates Russian into English. . . .

[3] From *Effects of Automation on Employment and Manpower Planning,* statement by Charles C. Killingsworth, professor of labor and industrial relations, Michigan State University, on June 14-15, 1960, before the Subcommittee on Employment and Manpower of the United States Senate Committee on Labor and Public Welfare. (1960-61 Reprint Series no 37) Labor and Industrial Relations Center. Michigan State University. East Lansing. '60. Reprinted by permission.

Most metalworking industries are likely to be considerably affected by a new technique which teams up computers and mechanical or electronic control devices. This technique is called numerical control. In some ways the basic principle is remotely comparable to the old-fashioned player piano. It works roughly this way: Technicians take engineering drawings or even rough sketches and, using a special "computer language," feed information into the computer. The computer makes the necessary calculations and works out detailed instructions which are recorded on tape or punch cards. Then the tape or cards are simply plugged into a control unit on a machine tool, and the rest of the operation is completely automatic. The control unit can even inspect the work of the machine tool and make instantaneous corrections while the work is in process. The tape or card can be used over and over. The significance of numerical control lies in its ability to reduce machine time and increase quality, especially on complex operations. The cost of one large aircraft part was reduced from $18,500 per unit by conventional methods to $1,950 by numerical control, a reduction of almost 90 per cent in cost. The machining time on a part used in electrical manufacturing was reduced from sixty hours to forty-five minutes, and the rejection rate dropped from 50 per cent with human operators to 2 per cent with numerical control. . . . United States Steel opened a new rolling mill in Chicago which utilizes numerical control techniques. One authority has estimated that on about 90 per cent of present-day metalworking operations numerical control will be found feasible.

We are just beginning to explore the capabilities of computers. Experimental computers have been trained to compose original music, to play chess and checkers. The checkers experiment was especially interesting and significant, because the computer was also programed to learn from experience—the more games it played the better it got, until it was finally unbeatable, at least by humans. What would happen if two of these unbeatable computers met each other is interesting to speculate.

These examples could be multiplied. Computers have many advantages over mere humans, of course. Computers never tire, never forget, and work thousands of times as fast as men. There is another characteristic of computers that may be the most important of all. What one computer has "learned" can in many cases be "taught" to another computer almost instantaneously and at virtually no cost. Thus, the initial programing of a computer for complex decision-making tasks may be very costly and time consuming, but replication of that programing may be rapid and inexpensive. I am sure that I need not underscore the contrast with the time and cost (as well as travail) involved in transferring knowledge from one human being to another.

Three Aspects of Technological Development

At the risk of considerable oversimplification, we might say that mechanization up to now has involved three main strands, each related to the other, and perhaps not completely distinguishable from the other. One of these strands has been the substitution of mechanical power for the muscle power of humans or animals. The steam engine and electric motors are examples of that. Another strand has been specialization, breaking down work processes into small and smaller fragments to improve the efficiency of men and machines. I think that historians may record that the automobile assembly line represented a peak of that development in specialization. I think the third strand is automation, the development of mechanical control and thought. . . .

Now I think this third strand, automation, means the substitution of mechanical brains for human brains.

A great deal of the significance of automation lies in the fact that the enormous gains in output and accuracy that result from most kinds of automation are achieved largely by freeing machines from the limitations that have been previously imposed on them by the feeble, sluggish brains and perceptions of man.

I do not want to imply that any computer today is the over-all equal of an average human brain. I like to believe that there are a great many aspects of judgment and creativity and perhaps we might add compassion that will always distinguish most men from machines. But I don't think we should forget either that the scientists are constantly at work improving the machines.

Effects of Automation

Now I turn to the effects of automation. Despite the millions of words that have been spoken and written on this subject in the last ten years, any careful student must admit that we have much too little solid information concerning automation to be sure about its ultimate effects. I do believe that we know enough at least to question some of the widely held assumptions concerning the social and economic effects of automation.

Indeed, I contend that we may endanger some of the potential benefits of automation if we fail to investigate with great care the validity of some beliefs which a great many people apparently regard as little less than gospel truth. . . .

[One] notion that I think we should reexamine is the one which one hears so frequently, that inventions and other mechanical improvements always create more jobs than they eliminate.

Number of Jobs Affected by Automation

Some people seem to believe that there is a great law of nature which guarantees that any man who loses his job to a machine will always find another job elsewhere, if he only tries to do it. This belief may have been encouraged by the findings of numerous case studies that have been made of the installation of automated equipment.

Almost all of these studies have reported that no individual employed by the company that was making the installation lost his job as a result of installing automated equipment. Then many people also cite the example of the automobile industry in the first half of this century as a historical comparison.

That industry pioneered a great many labor-saving improvements, including of course the assembly line, one of the greatest developments in production techniques during the first half of the twentieth century. But despite these improvements, the automobile industry expanded its employment enormously during that fifty-year period.

The theory of automatic reabsorption of displaced labor obviously has a degree of validity. But I doubt that even its original nineteenth-century proponents would argue that it would hold true in all times, all places, and all circumstances. They certainly would have conceded that it is a long-run not a short-run theory.

And they also would have conceded that it assumes certain important conditions, particularly mobility of labor and full employment in the economy generally.

The fact is that a substantial part of the cost savings from automation usually results from displacement of labor. It is distinctly to the credit of American management and labor that they have cooperated, in most of the cases that have been studied, to find other jobs in the same company for those who have been replaced by machines.

The normal turnover in the company quite frequently has made it unnecessary to lay anybody off. But, from the standpoint of society, the net result of that process may well be simply to shift the burden of unemployment from the man who already had a job with the company to the man who doesn't get hired by that company.

Or the burden may fall on the man who gets laid off in the next recession and never gets called back, which has obviously happened increasingly in our last three recessions.

In a strong growth industry, like the automobile industry from 1900 to 1950, rising demand for its products may more than offset the labor-saving effects of mechanization. But the fact is that we seem to have a shortage of major growth industries at the present time. . . .

Blue-collar employment in manufacturing has actually been falling off in the past few years, even though output has been rising, due in very large measure to automation. It is significant that much more than a proportionate share of the hard core unemployment in our distressed areas is composed of workers whose last job was in manufacturing. . . .

[Another] difficulty with the automatic reabsorption theory is that the mobility of an unemployed worker is severely limited. . . . Most important of all is that long-run adjustments may very well take a lifetime.

People must live in the short run as well as in the economist's long run. Perhaps the classic comment on this point was made by J. M. Keynes who commented that in the long run we are all dead. . . .

Will Automation Come Slowly?

Another notion that I feel we must question is the idea that automation will come slowly. This perhaps is based on an examination of historical trends of the past.

It is true that more than one hundred years was needed for the steam engine to be widely adopted in industry. It took more than fifty years for electric power to come into general use. Some present-day computer installations require years of planning. Moreover, business and industry certainly will not scrap many billions of dollars' worth of existing equipment overnight.

Even if there were an incentive to do so, replacements of that kind would obviously be limited by the ability of the economy to produce the new equipment. But I think we must look at the other side of the picture.

The cost of automation equipment like computers is being constantly reduced, and the number produced is being expanded. I might interpolate that a great deal of this progress is very recent.

There has been a trend toward miniaturization of components, which has both increased the power and decreased the size of computers, and is likely to decrease their cost as well. There do not appear to be any insuperable shortages of manpower or of materials which would stand in the way of a large expansion of output of automation equipment over the next few years, if the demand for it were to rise.

Such a rise in demand may be spurred by powerful incentives. One aircraft manufacturer, for example, reports that a large new machine which operates on principles of numerical control and which cost $500,000 pays for itself in savings in about ninety days. If a $500,000 machine can pay for itself in ninety days, obviously there is an extremely strong incentive to borrow money for ninety days in order to acquire that machine. . . .

The savings don't have to be as dramatic as that in order to induce businessmen to replace perfectly good capital equipment with the latest thing or a later thing. I would cite the example of the airlines, which today are spending billions of dollars in order to buy jet aircraft, even though they now have hundreds of older propeller-driven planes that are still completely airworthy.

The point is that the venturesome competitor who invests in the newest equipment may be able to achieve such great savings and to attract customers so powerfully that other firms in the industry will be compelled to invest in the same or better equipment simply in order to remain in business. . . .

I would say . . . that something like . . . [this] seems to have happened in the automobile industry. Even the smallest and financially weakest company in the industry has spent millions of dollars on automation equipment.

In an automobile plant, an engine line that is five years old is obsolete from the competitive standpoint. In some industries, the progress of automation may very well be extremely slow, as so many people assume. But I think it is erroneous and dangerous to exclude the possibility that automation will progress quite rapidly in others. . . .

The matter of speed is a crucial factor in measuring impact. The introduction of the steam engine had many disruptive side effects; imagine the impact if its use had become general in twenty years instead of a hundred years.

Every labor-saving invention necessitates some redistribution of the labor force. The labor market, on which we rely for such redistribution, is likely to work slowly and inefficiently when large numbers of people are involved. Millions of excess workers have been moved out of agriculture in the past few decades, but the farm labor supply is still greatly in excess of what is really needed to produce food and fiber for our nation.

The point is that our present institutional framework is much better able to handle change which comes slowly than that which comes rapidly. It is of great importance, therefore, that we try to judge how rapidly automation is moving. Too little effort of this kind is being made today.

AMERICAN NEGROES—A WASTED RESOURCE [4]

The Negro community in this country now includes more than 16 million persons. Few of these people are being utilized at a level which even approaches their capacity, either as manpower or as consumers. Both in the South and in the North their

[4] From article by J. J. Morrow, vice president in charge of personnel relations, Pitney-Bowes, Inc. *Harvard Business Review*. 35:65-74. Ja.-F. '57. Reprinted by permission.

contribution to the nation's economy is far below what it could and should be.

Julius A. Thomas, industrial relations director of the National Urban League, estimates that more than 1 million Negro workers are currently underemployed—that 500,000 of them could be upgraded almost immediately, while more than 800,000 could be quickly trained so that they could accept added responsibilities. . . .

Thomas bases his estimate on figures like these:

Less than 3 per cent of Negro males outside the South are professional or technical personnel, as opposed to more than 8 per cent of the white population.

While 11 per cent of white men are managers, officials, and proprietors, only 3 per cent of the Negroes in the country hold such jobs.

More than 70 per cent of employed Negroes are working in the lowest nonfarm job classifications in the North and the West; fewer than 33 per cent of white men are in these occupations.

Only 9 per cent of the Negro women outside the South are clerical and sales workers, though over 40 per cent of employed white women hold such assignments. . . .

Industry has been taking increasing advantage of Negro manpower during the past ten or fifteen years. When . . . figures on Negro employment since 1940 are set against those drawn from the first eight decades of the Negro's legal freedom, the change is striking. Two world wars, government antidiscrimination programs, industrial manpower shortages, and the shift of the Negro population from the South to the North have all been contributing factors. In contrast with the post-World War I experience, Negro workers hired during World War II held their jobs after the war was over. . . .

It is true that some companies still do not use any nonwhite people at all, but the more important fact is that a great many more fail to utilize them to their fullest. Such firms do not train or promote Negroes. When they do employ nonwhite personnel, they automatically place them in the most menial tasks—without regard for the actual or latent talent they are wasting. Thus, though there has been some upgrading during this period of expansion, Negroes generally are not serving industry to their top potential. . . .

In the South

It may come as a surprise to learn that in the South a Negro's chance of working in the areas that are generally least available to him—as professionals, managers, officials, or proprietors—is actually greater than it is in the North. However, this is no paradox. In fact, the explanation is simple: the growing size and prosperity of the Negro communities in southern cities has encouraged the growth of Negro enterprises serving members of their own race.

At the same time, skilled Negroes have been an important part of the South's construction industry, and many have found employment in it and in the flourishing automobile industry in recent years. A few branches of northern corporations and the Federal Government have led the way in several cities in the South to demonstrate that greater opportunities can be successfully and profitably extended to Negroes.

The fact remains that, in spite of the gains made, the major increases in nonfarm employment of Negro men have been at the lower levels. For instance, only one in eight is employed as a white-collar or skilled nonagricultural worker, compared to one out of every two white men. In 1950, there were fewer than 500 Negro engineers in the South, compared to well over 100,000 white engineers. As for other professional men, most have been limited to Negro institutions; two thirds are clergymen and teachers serving only other Negroes.

Negro men in manufacturing are employed mainly as laborers, material handlers, or janitors. Except in foundries or sawmills, few Negroes hold any kind of production jobs—particularly jobs on the production line, which is the major route to skilled and supervisory positions in manufacturing. One example is the automobile industry in the South, where in 1950 more than 10,000 white men were working as operatives, but fewer than 350 Negroes.

Female employment has expanded more rapidly than male employment in the urban South, but the opportunities for Negro women are even more severely restricted. They are concentrated in the poorest jobs in the food processing, tobacco, garment, and a few other industries.

In the North

As for the North and the West, the problems of the Negro here are as varied as the communities within these regions. All in all, however, the difficulties are still major. The percentage of Negro men working above the semiskilled level is only slightly higher than in the South, and the general pattern of under-employment parallels that of the South.

The northern Negro's most conspicuous advantage is that he has a greater opportunity to obtain clerical or sales work. But the proportion of Negroes at the bottom of the occupational ladder—laborers and service workers—is only slightly smaller than in the South.

Fewer than one fourth of the Negroes outside the South are employed in nonmanual occupations or in skilled jobs, as opposed to more than three fifths of the white nonfarm workers.

In skilled work, the Negro is able to enter a wider variety of occupations in the North, and his chances are better of finding employment in semiskilled jobs that may lead to skilled or supervisory work.

Negro women in the North have made great advances also, especially in clerical and sales work. But in the North as in the South, and in 1950 as in 1940, the outstanding fact about Negro women working in cities is that most of them are service workers —servants, cleaning women, waitresses, hospital attendants, cooks. Fewer than one in ten had clerical or sales jobs, compared to two out of five white women.

Manpower Shortage

These attitudes—unwillingness to employ Negroes at all, hesitancy to place them in more skilled jobs, and reluctance to give them the advantages of training and promotion enjoyed by their white counterparts—are particularly shortsighted when placed against the background of a severe shortage in skilled manpower throughout this country. . . .

It is true that some effect of this manpower shortage has been felt in the Negro community, especially in the North. It is now "open season" on jobs for trained Negroes in the scientific and technical fields. Except in the South, it is also much easier for able office personnel to find suitable employment. Negroes are moving ahead as health technicians, laboratory assistants, and social workers. But the impact all the way down the line hardly makes a dent in the serious needs which America faces.

From an over-all standpoint, then, the picture is a mixed one which shows some improvement in recent years. But there is nothing remotely approaching maximum use of Negro actual or potential skills, either at the top of the industrial hierarchy or at the bottom. Furthermore, there is no reason to believe that further development will "just happen," without concerted and conscientious efforts on the part of industry to capitalize on this reservoir of undeveloped talent.

Depressed Purchasing Power

This waste of skill—of people—is only part of the problem. The purchasing power of the Negro community is way below what it would be were Negroes receiving the same remuneration and opportunity as whites of equal ability.

The median income of all U.S. Negro families is 56 per cent of the income of white families—$2,410 a year as opposed to $4,339. In the South, where conditions are worse, the median income of Negro families is only about 49 per cent of what white families take in. In 1950, average individual earnings for the Negro were $1,200, while his white counterpart was making $2,600. Even where the Negro fares best—in the northeastern urban communities—his income reaches only 67 per cent of the white average.

The well-educated Negro has improved his position considerably since 1940, but Negroes still earn far less than whites who have had the same amount of education. Throughout the country, Negro college graduates earned less in 1949 than did whites who had attended—but not graduated from—high school. And the more education the individuals have acquired, the greater the discrepancy between white and Negro salaries tends to be.

There are many reasons for these figures, some of which center on the matter of underdevelopment of skills and underemployment as discussed earlier. That a number of companies still fail to hire Negroes at any level is only the most obvious cause.

More serious is the fact that, for the most part, the better educated nonwhite man must apply himself exclusively to the service of his fellows in Negro communities if he wishes to make full use of his talents. He must voluntarily choose segregation and work with members of his own race in professional, social, or educational capacities. Needless to say, such positions do not generally carry large salaries. This lack of opportunity at the highest levels depresses the scale all the way down. Furthermore, it chops off the incentive to work hard, move ahead, earn more money, and increase the standard of living which is such an important dynamic of the American system.

At the lower end of the range, the ratio of unemployment among Negroes always runs higher than among whites—about 5 per cent for Negroes as against 3 per cent for whites.

It is not enough to point to the examples of exceptional men and women in specialized fields as proof that there are no longer any opportunities closed to Negroes. Difficult as it is for a brilliant and talented Negro to reach his proper level, great ability, coupled with the urge toward achievement common among unusual men, is often enough to push through any kind of obstacle. The average person has no such tools; and it is the great majority of Negroes, in between the unqualified and the exceptional, who make up the unattractive over-all picture of the Negro's status.

Thus, the opportunities for the Negro—and his income—are limited by devices ranging from clear-cut bans to discouragement. Lack of the chance to receive advanced training, denial of an equal chance at promotions, assignment to the most menial tasks, lower wage scales, closed doors at the top—all combine to drive down the standard of living for these 16 million people. . . .

Limitations of the Community

It can be honestly argued that the Negro community as a whole is not up to the white population in education, training, health, vigor, and other qualities that a modern industrial society demands of its workers and managers. While more than 65,000 Negro men and women are graduated annually from the nation's high schools, and about 10,000 receive diplomas from colleges, these figures are far below the percentage for the white population. The improvement since 1940 is substantial, but so is the lag. At the . . . [1950] census, three out of every five young Negro men in the South had no high school education; and one out of four in the North found himself with the same lack of training.

If the educational level of Negroes were raised to that of whites in the North and West, the number of Negro high school graduates would rise annually (based on 1950 figures) from 64,800 to 157,800. The figure on college graduates would rise from 9,400 to 23,200. But, as we well know, the problem goes beyond simple numbers. The best authorities, even in the South, concede that all too often the quality of the education given Negroes falls below that available to whites.

Home environment, living conditions, and levels of health—reflecting, in turn, the results of low income, poor opportunities, and segregation in housing—also handicap the Negro in his attempt to compete successfully on the open market for better jobs and higher pay.

However, it should be pointed out that these weaknesses are environmental in character. There is *no* evidence to indicate that the Negro cannot be just as effectively integrated into a modern industial society as his white counterpart, given equality of training, background, and experience. The progress in the past few years bears this out. Furthermore, a vicious circle has set in here. As Dr. Eli Ginzberg pointed out in his book entitled *The Negro Potential*:

> For the Negro population to be able to compete on an equal basis for professional, scientific, managerial, skilled, and other desirable jobs will require a revolution in all levels of Negro education, and beyond

this, in the values and aspirations, the living conditions, and the community environments of large groups in the Negro population. All of this, in turn, depends in large part on the opportunities of Negroes to earn larger incomes.

GUIDE TO CHOICE OF CAREER[5]

General Occupational Fields

In order to make fair evaluations in terms of job opportunities . . . it is necessary to know something about the total work world. There are many thousands of job possibilities which can be somewhat roughly classified into nine broad areas: professional; semiprofessional; farmers and farm managers; proprietors, managers, and officials; clerical, sales, and kindred workers; craftsmen; operatives; laborers; and workers in services such as gas stations, beauty parlors, laundries, etc.

Professional careers require college graduation in almost all cases; in some professions the trend is in the direction of graduate work beyond the Bachelor of Science (B.S.) or Bachelor of Arts (B.A.) degrees commonly given after four years of undergraduate training. Advanced degrees are usually called the master's degree and the doctorate. The professional field includes such occupational titles as accountant, architect, clergyman, dentist, engineer, lawyer, librarian, nurse, personnel worker, physician, social worker, and teacher—to name only a few occupations which are designated as professional.

Semiprofessional careers often require college graduation or some college training, or work in a technical school. The trend is toward demanding a college degree in many areas. The semiprofessional field includes such titles as airline pilot, designer, draftsman, medical service worker, photographer, radio operator, and technician.

Farmers and farm managers encompass a large number of people who rent farms as tenants, own their own farms, or manage the farms of others. There are no definite educational requirements but minimum training for today's farm owners and tenants should be high school graduation with emphasis on study

[5] From *You and Your Career*, pamphlet by H. Alan Robinson, assistant professor of reading and education, Hofstra College, prepared under the supervision of the editors of *Collier's Encyclopedia*. Library and Educational Division. Crowell-Collier Publishing Company. 640 Fifth Ave. New York 19. '61. p 1-4. Reprinted by permission.

of agricultural methods and problems. Some college training is recommended. Farm managers are often required to have college degrees.

Proprietors, managers, and officials have various kinds of training, depending on their particular fields of endeavor. College training is needed or desirable in some cases, although a high school education is often acceptable. Job titles include such categories as advertising agent, buyer and department head in retail stores, foreman and supervisor, hotel manager, postmaster, public official, purchasing agent, railroad conductor, store manager, theater manager, and numerous other titles which could be included in this category.

Clerical, sales, and kindred workers include such job titles as bookkeeper, cashier, clerk, insurance agent, mail carrier, real estate agent, salesman, secretary, stenographer, telephone operator, and typist. High school graduation is usually either required or preferred. In some cases it is also desirable to have some business or technical school training before entering these fields.

Craftsmen must usually be high school graduates who will continue their education with formal apprenticeships or on-the-job training programs. In a number of cases it is preferable for the prospective craftsman to enter a technical school following high school graduation. Titles include baker, blacksmith, carpenter, compositor, electrician, glazier, jeweler, locomotive engineer, machinist, painter, plumber, and many other types of craftsmen.

Operatives are often required to be high school graduates, although this is not essential. Companies hiring operatives usually sponsor their own training programs or, in a few cases, enter into formal apprenticeship agreements with new employees. Operatives have job titles such as chauffeur, laundry worker, miner, railroad brakeman and switchman, telephone and telegraph lineman, welder, and various others.

Service worker is a classification given to a multitude of job titles when the job emphasis is on servicing individuals or the community. For some of these jobs there are no educational requirements at all—such as for a housekeeper, laundress, domestic worker, custodian, porter, usher, waiter and waitress—although an elementary school education and beyond is invariably preferable. Some jobs require high school or vocational school graduation and/or specialized schooling, such as fireman, guard, policeman, soldier, barber, beautician, and cook.

Laborers are so classified when the bulk of the work on the job requires physical effort or strength. In most cases there are no educational requirements or special schooling needs; most training takes place on the job itself. Job titles in this category include farm laborer, fisherman, gardener, garage laborer, longshoreman, lumberman, and teamster. . . .

Occupational Information

In exploring the work world it is vital that the student know how to marshal the facts. He may learn a good deal from counselors, parents, people working in various fields, and representatives of a variety of occupations sent to the high school or college. It is imperative that he learn how to read and evaluate published occupational literature and that he know how to study an occupation, through reading or actual observation, if he is to use the information to aid him in the selection of a career. Along with his search for facts, the student must evaluate the occupation in terms of answers to specific questions:

Importance of the work. What contributions has the occupation made to mankind? Do you consider the work vital and important?

Origin and history. What kind of progress has the occupation made as it has developed? Does its past history point to a successful future?

Employment trend. Are workers in this field in demand today? Are beginners wanted? Will employment increase or decrease within the next ten or twenty years? Why?

Nature of the work. How is the occupation defined according to the *Dictionary of Occupational Titles?* (The *Dictionary of Occupational Titles* is published by the United States Government Printing Office and is usually available in any library or guidance office.) What are the exact duties? Do they change in different situations? How do the duties measure up to your concepts?

Personal qualifications. What are the physical requirements for the job, if any? Do you need particular aptitudes and abilities? Do you possess them?

Preparation. How much training is essential and how much is preferred? How long and how costly is the training? What does the training include? Do you need experience in addition to training? Do you need a license or certificate in order to go to work?

Entrance. How is the first job obtained? What do you do when you begin?

Advancement. What are the possibilities for advancement? To what positions can you advance? How much further training or experience do you need for advancement?

Earnings. What are the average beginning earnings? What is the average range of earnings for all workers? What is the average range in the community or plant where you might seek employment? How much can you earn after five years of experience? Ten years? Twenty-five years? What are the top earnings for those with exceptional ability?

Number and distribution of workers. About how many people are employed? What are the opportunities for men and women? Are there job opportunities throughout the United States?

Advantages and disadvantages. Are people satisfied with their jobs? Why? What are the chief factors named as advantages and as disadvantages? Do these factors seem like advantages or disadvantages to you?

Sources of further information. Are there professional associations, labor organizations, and other agencies which may be contacted for additional information about the occupation?

[The pamphlet from which this selection is taken is an excellent source of career information. The 1961 edition gives up-to-date answers to the above questions for 121 careers. Other sources are listed in the bibliography.—Ed.]

MILITARY SERVICE AS A CAREER[6]

Jet Age, Atomic Age, Missile Age, Space Age—no matter what you call this age of ours, it is without question an Age of Opportunity.

One opportunity, open to young men and women, is a career in the military service. Young men in particular are almost

[6] From article by Brigadier General S. F. Giffin, USAF. *Senior Scholastic.* 76:11-13. F. 10, '60. From *Senior Scholastic.* © 1960 by Scholastic Magazines, Inc. Reprinted by permission.

obliged to consider a military career, for by law many of them will have to spend at least six years—divided variously between active and reserve duty—in one of our five armed services.

Taking time out to serve this obligation in our country need not cause any delay in getting on with a career. For the armed forces of the United States today afford a chance to learn and practice in one manner or another virtually every trade, occupation, or profession to be found in civilian life. And never in the history of any nation have the armed forces offered more inducements to the young man or woman to choose military service itself as a career.

Types of Jobs

The nation's armed services—Army, Navy, Air Force, Marine Corps, and Coast Guard—today contain more than 250 "career fields" embracing more than two thousand specialist jobs. These deal with things like electronics, guided missiles, and nuclear weapons. Or others, perhaps not so unusual but nonetheless vital: engineering, photography, transportation, aviation, medicine, communications. This list is long.

Assignment to a specific career field depends both on the aptitudes of the individual and on the needs of the service. But the man who enlists, as opposed to the man who waits to be drafted, can select the particular service that appeals to him, and the service will do everything possible to place him in the work he prefers and for which he is qualified. The Army and Navy even provide an opportunity for selecting a career field before enlistment. If a candidate passes appropriate aptitude and physical tests, the Army will guarantee that, upon completion of basic training, he will be assigned to his chosen field.

But whether by specific choice or otherwise, the man who serves will have the opportunity to learn and practice a practical and valuable trade or profession. . . .

The so-called "combat arms"—the Navy's fighting ships, the Marines, the Air Force's combat commands, the Army's infantry, artillery, armor, and combat engineers—still form the hard core of our armed forces. Yet so highly developed have become the weapons, equipment, and combat methods of these branches that serving in them is no longer a matter of just marching and shooting. Today's infantryman, for example, must know much more than how to aim a rifle and pull the trigger. He may have to operate and maintain expensive and complicated machine guns, mortars, or anti-tank missiles. Or he may be in charge of motor vehicles, radios, or intricate telephone systems. Any of these or other jobs has a related counterpart in civilian life.

Opportunities for Women

Nor is the young woman who looks to the services for a career neglected. She may serve either in the WAC (Women's Army Corps), WAF (Women in the Air Force), WAVES (Women in the Navy), Women Marines, or as a nurse or medical specialist. . . .

A young woman may become an X-ray technician, a secretary, cryptographer, personnel specialist, laboratory technician, or one of hundreds of other specialists who release men to the combat arms or to other physically demanding jobs. . . .

The services can offer this variety of assignments for two reasons: First, the idea that every serviceman carries a gun and meets the enemy face to face is out of date, although they all must be prepared to do so if the need arises. In World War II, for example, for every soldier who manned a front-line position, at least six others stood behind him, performing essential and often complicated supporting tasks. Because of the technological advances since World War II, this figure has been reduced while the tasks have multiplied in complexity.

Second, the job of the armed forces is not all fighting wars. Their main job is to be *prepared* to fight, and by being prepared, to deter war from starting. But as a corollary of this job, the armed forces now, as in the past, contribute in countless ways to the betterment of our civilization.

It was the military, for example, that led the way in discovery and exploration of the American West. It was the Army that built the Panama Canal. It was military doctors who licked the dread disease of yellow fever and in recent years pioneered in the use of sulfa drugs, penicillin, and blood plasma. The Navy has explored the Arctic and the Antarctic. . . . [Recently] the Navy sent atomic submarines under the icecap of the north polar region on voyages that may lead to shortened sea routes for commercial use. Commercial aviation owes many a debt to the Air Force. The Army, Navy and Air Force are all actively engaged in exploring space. The skills of mass movement of troops and supplies by helicopter developed by the Marine Corps are used extensively in aiding disaster victims. The Coast Guard, among other duties, serves as the nation's sea-rescue service, and its weather ships provide information for transoceanic ships and planes. Thus the man who chooses the military for a career and possesses the necessary aptitudes and ability works in the very forefront of the nation's advances in innumerable fields not traditionally looked upon as military pursuits.

Career Inducements

Patriotism has always been and continues to be a strong inducement for choosing a military career. Now there are additional strong inducements. . . .

In recognition of the new responsibilities, the Congress of the United States has increased military pay and allowances. While the recruit may earn for a while no more than $78 actual cash per month, he will receive many fringe benefits that would cost him much in civilian life.

An enlisted man gets his housing and food. He gets medical and dental care for himself and medical care for his dependents. He receives a complete set of uniforms. He has access to recreational facilities as good or better than those in most towns and on most college campuses. He can purchase food and personal and household items through commissaries and exchanges and attend movies and other entertainments at reduced prices.

He comes under both the social security program and the military retirement plan. Under the latter, he can retire after only twenty years' service at half his monthly pay; after thirty years, at three fourths his monthly pay. . . . Thus a man who enlists at the minimum age of seventeen conceivably could draw more than $200 retirement pay at the age of thirty-seven, while he is still young enough to begin a second full-time career. To obtain similar benefits in civilian life would require an investment of $50,000 at 5 per cent interest.

The serviceman's pay rises with promotion to higher grades and through pay increases within grade. He can rise in less than twenty years *as an enlisted man* to a monthly base pay, exclusive of all other pay and benefits, as high as $420. Top enlisted pay is $440. He may earn as much as . . . [$60] a month extra for particular proficiency in his job, as much as $105 a month for hazardous duty, and as much as $22.50 a month for overseas duty. If married, he may receive subsistence and housing allowances instead of Government furnished rations and quarters, adding as much as $130 a month to his cash income. Each time he reenlists he receives a bonus which, over the course of a full career in the service, may amount to as much as $2,000. Almost all pay except base pay is exempt from income tax.

Almost all these benefits can be classified as financial, something few young people planning a career can afford to ignore. But other considerations also enter the picture, often with even greater emphasis.

One consideration is the sense of accomplishment that an individual can expect from the work he performs. The man or woman who chooses a military career can know without qualification that he is performing a real and essential service to his fellow man and to his country.

Educational Programs

Another consideration is perhaps of even greater importance to the high school senior, particularly the senior who for various reasons does not choose, or cannot go, to college. The thinking high school graduate will know that he still has much to learn. Here is where the military services can provide assistance remarkable in scope and opportunity, for the services today have become one of this nation's biggest and most comprehensive educational establishments.

The services together maintain more than 250 basic schools, almost all of which prepare a man or woman to enter a specialized career field. Once established in a career field, he then may go on to further training in more advanced schools. The Army alone gave advanced training in a recent year to some 150,000 officers and enlisted members in thirty-six Army-operated schools. The other services have similar programs.

There are also programs to assist the high school graduate obtain a formal college education. If he intends to make a career in the service and can qualify, he may take a four-year course at one of the service academies—the Military Academy at West Point, the Naval Academy at Annapolis, the Air Force Academy at Colorado Springs, or the Coast Guard Academy at New London. He will graduate with a Bachelor of Science degree, plus a commission as a second lieutenant or ensign.

If he goes to college, he may enroll in Army, Navy, or Air Force Reserve Officers' Training Corps (ROTC) programs, receive $27 a month during his junior and senior years, and earn a commission. If he can meet the requirements of a special ROTC program conducted by the Navy, called NROTC (Regular), the Navy will give him $50 a month and subsidize his . . . education. The Marine Corps Platoon Leaders Class gives military training leading to a commission in two six-week periods during college summers.

Other programs offered in cooperation with some three hundred colleges and universities are open to men and women on active duty. Any serviceman or woman may take correspondence courses leading to a college degree. These are offered at a small fee under auspices of the United States Armed Forces Institute (USAFI). Those who qualify can take courses during off-duty hours either at nearby campuses or on the military base itself, for which the service may pay up to 75 per cent of tuition fees. The services also have programs to provide college-level training in science and engineering.

In offering programs like these, the services obviously appreciate that the educated man or woman can better perform today's complex military tasks. Yet before moving to technical assignments, every soldier, sailor, airman, and marine must master the fundamentals of military service. And certain strictly military duties will always remain. There may even be temporary assignments under relatively unpleasant conditions, something every man must face from time to time, even in civilian life. But the fact remains—once a man has mastered the basic mechanics of military service, whether infantryman, boatswain's mate, or electronics specialist, his career horizon stretches wide. Opportunities abound in the enlisted ranks. However, if an enlisted man wants to become a warrant officer or a commissioned officer, the doors are open through hard work and study.

III. MARRIAGE

EDITOR'S INTRODUCTION

It is generally agreed that Americans marry earlier today than they did a generation ago. Half of all women are now married by the age of twenty and half of all men by the age of twenty-three. The literature on "early marriage" usually concentrates on either high school or college marriage, thus distinguishing in a general way between two different age categories and two different kinds of problems. The first two selections given in this section deal primarily with college marriage. The well-known anthropologist Margaret Mead comments on contributing causes of early marriage and deplores the pattern of "fur-lined domesticity" which young people often adopt. Lester A. Kirkendall, professor of family life at the University of Oregon, focuses specifically on the problems which beset student couples and offers suggestions to both students and the college for improving conditions for campus marriage.

In the third article, Henry Bowman, associate professor of sociology at the University of Texas, describes some changes that have occurred in American marriage in the past fifty years or so. Although the next selection, by Nelson N. Foote, former director of the Family Study Center of the University of Chicago, is couched in fairly specialized terms, it will yield much helpful information to careful readers. Dr. Foote outlines in detail several areas in which the status of married women has changed and points out that those women who adopt new (and as yet not fully defined) roles often suffer from uncertainty and self-doubt. There is much material in general magazines and books which deals with the subject of new roles for women. The fact that expectations for men at home and at work have also altered is less often mentioned explicitly. "New Burdens of Masculinity" by Helen Mayer Hacker, who teaches in the Department of Home and Family Life at Columbia University Teachers College, examines the tensions experienced by men as they seek to define and embody new masculine roles.

Two of the major problems frequently mentioned by married couples relate to disagreement about finances and in-laws. Judson T. and Mary G. Landis, well-known commentators in the family life field, discuss some factors which contribute to conflict over family income and expenditure. In "How to Get Along with Any In-Law," Evelyn Millis Duvall, who carried out one of the first major studies of in-law attitudes, surveys in-law relationships and offers advice on how to improve them. The final article, on interfaith marriage, is particularly significant for modern young people, who are no longer prevented by force of tradition or lack of opportunity from considering marriage with persons of different religious backgrounds.

A NEW LOOK AT EARLY MARRIAGES [1]

Q. Dr. Mead, are teen-age marriages increasing?

A. This is a trend that is more pronounced in the United States than anywhere else, I think. But there is a slight trend toward marriages at the student age level in the Western democracies as a whole. . . .

Q. Is marriage in college now commonplace?

A. It's becoming so in most of the country, except in colleges that are still one-sex colleges, and haven't yet got any married students' quarters. Especially in the big state universities and nonresidential colleges in cities, student marriages are becoming more and more frequent. And, in professional schools such as law and medicine, where twenty-five years ago hardly any students were married, today marriages are commonplace.

Q. How early in college are marriages occurring? As early as the freshman or sophomore year?

A. Very often, for girls. It's not quite that early for boys. In general, we have a notion that boys ought to be one or two years older than their wives, and no more.

This means that many girls, by the end of their sophomore year, are engaged to boys who are seniors.

Q. So the girls are often teen-agers?

[1] From interview with Margaret Mead, associate curator of ethnology, American Museum of Natural History, and adjunct professor of anthropology, Columbia University. *U.S. News & World Report.* 48:80-86. Je. 6, '60. Reprinted from *U.S. News & World Report,* published at Washington. Copyright 1960 United States News Publishing Corporation.

A. Yes. Of course, this "teen-age" idea is pretty new, you know. One hundred years ago, young people of age eighteen to twenty were men and women.

Today we have headlines like "Nineteen-year-old, milk-drinking, teen-age murderer." Our attempt to deal with juveniles differently from the way we've dealt with adults under the law has now introduced this term "teen-ager," and technically you're a teen-ager until you're twenty. But the real image of teen-agers ought to be somewhere around age fifteen to sixteen. . . .

Q. What seems to account for this trend to get married while still in college?

A. There are a whole lot of different causes that have been identified.

For the last twenty-five or thirty years we've had a great deal of agitation along the lines that adolescents are sexually mature, and that a society that denies them a sex life until sometime late in their twenties—or, in some societies, even into their thirties—is going against nature.

Now, from time to time we're in favor of nature and at other times we're against it. As far as sex is concerned today, we think we're in favor of nature, and we think sex is good for you and you ought to have it, under licensed and domestic conditions. . . .

This general notion about sex—which has developed in this country in the last twenty-five years—means, of course, we disapprove now of any form of single blessedness. We suspect any form of single-minded dedication. We are running very short of religious orders on which many important institutions in this country have been based. We have to import nuns from other countries, for example, to teach schools and run hospitals because this whole country now believes that marriage—that regular sex life inside marriage—is physiologically necessary for everyone. This has been one factor in these college marriages.

Another factor is that everybody is doing things younger today. They're not only getting married younger. They're piloting planes younger. If we look at what our young men are expected to do in war, we realize that we're putting a tremendous strain on young people.

This pressing down on young people, into premature responsibilities, is not confined only to marriage.

Q. Are junior high school dances and other organized social affairs in the schools part of this pressure?

A. Yes, they're very much part of the pressure, especially where people insist on the dances being limited to the junior high school, so that, instead of the girl who is a senior in junior high school going out with the boys of the senior high schools, she is going out with a boy of her own age in the junior high school. And she's beginning to be part of the pressure that's put on him steadily, that he ought to be beginning this mating process so early.

Q. Long before he understands what it's all about?

A. Yes, and at a time when he really shouldn't be having anything to do with girls at all, in most cases.

Q. When should he start?

A. He should start when he wants to, but not when society puts a pressure on him.

Boys should probably not starting courting girls until they have got their growth; until they have some sense of themselves as people; and until a girl a couple of years younger than they are is old enough to be courted.

Q. Do you believe the boy should be a year or two older than the girl?

A. At least two years older—I'd like to say more, but I don't see where it could fit into the American culture pattern—because the girl is so much more socially mature than the boy. . . .

Of course, one can only talk in averages, and it's important to recognize that you can't make judgments for any individual case by talking about an average.

Some sixteen-year-old boys are older than some twenty-four-year-old boys: more mature and able to do what they want. And some twelve-year-old girls are more grown up than their own mothers will ever be.

Q. Besides the emphasis on youth and sex, does anything else encourage these early marriages?

A. A third factor, I think, is that World War I, then the depression, then World War II and, finally, the Korean War have all discouraged the adult world—the people who are the parents of these kids. The parents have felt, "We want you to have some fun now. Take some enjoyment in life while you can get it. The future is totally uncertain."

The fear of atomic war—which is not being faced but is only being felt as a vague shadow—also is the sort of thing, just as war itself, that drives young people into "snatching" at happiness out of a sense that it's going to disappear if not taken.

Q. Have you talked to many college students?

A. I do a lot of lecturing at colleges. It's very, very striking the way the students feel that there is no time, that, if you aren't married and settled and have your career and a house before you're twenty-five—and some of them add you ought to have gone around the world, too—then somehow you're never going to get these things. . . .

Q. Which is more important in causing college marriages—the ideas that drive young people, or those that drive their parents?

A. The parents are driven into conniving with the youngsters in early dating, and early "going steady." They push the boys, as well as the girls, into courtship as early as possible and underwrite the marriage. . . .

At the same time, the young people have this feeling that they're living in a world where the future is very uncertain, so they might as well get what they can now—a husband, a wife, children, a house in the country.

Q. But who actually pushes for the marriages—the girls, or the boys, or the parents?

A. At this point everybody is pushing, to a degree. I think that it's still fair to say that the girl pushes more than the boy. A sixteen-year-old girl is far readier to marry than an eighteen-year-old boy. The way we've set things up now, dating begins in junior high school. It means that all through senior high school age . . . the last three years of high school, typically running up to age eighteen—all through this period the girls are pushing very hard to try to pin some boy down, and the boys get used to being pledged.

One of the reasons this happens is that the boys, you see, are very irresponsible until they have really attached themselves to a girl as a "steady," or until they're engaged. They're ruthless, exploitive and experimental. The girls have to spend their time keeping the boys in order because in America we expect them to say "No," so the girls have years of keeping boys in order, which is very wearing. And they want to get a boy they can trust pinned down so they don't have to work so hard to keep him in order.

Now, the boy, on the other hand, the minute he is pledged to a girl, becomes much more protective of her. And this is an important part of what is happening in our sex mores today.

Parents look at this and they realize that a boy who is going steady with a girl will take responsibility for the girl, and he won't be roaming from one town to another and one college to another like a wolf. And they don't particularly want their sons to be wolves.

At the same time, the parents of the girls realize that the minute the girl has a boy pinned down, she's safer. So both sets of parents get back of the marriage and push it.

I think the boys would still rather stay out of it if they could. . . .

Q. What do you think about the comment by a dean of students at a large U. S. college that college years are man-hunting and girl-hunting years anyway?

A. That is true in this country now. It isn't what those years have been in the history of civilization. It isn't quite certain we can call this civilization.

Q. What has happened? Is it considered old-fashioned to want a little time to think about marriage?

A. It's not fashionable at present, partly because in this country we've built this tremendous opposition to the intellectual by our high school system, and we've expanded our colleges to include more and more of the people that once went only through high school.

So we now have, actually, a high school standard of intellectual life on our college campuses, and this is combined with a very strict vocationalism among the young people—many of them already burdened with wives and children or husbands and children—who demand from colleges instead of a chance to think, or a chance to find themselves, a chance to become qualified for some job that will give them security and permit them to support this family that they either have or are going to have very soon.

Q. Is that desirable?

A. Intellectual life demands some kind of postponement of this early domesticity. Early domesticity has always been characteristic of most savages, of most peasants and of the urban poor. But most civilized societies—we have to remember—have only had a very small group of people who had any intellectual life, a very small group of people who went to universities.

In European history it has been the young men of the elite classes who were trained as philosophers, as priests, as statesmen and writers. They have been permitted to postpone responsibility while they had a chance in some reasonably protected environment to think, and to make friends with other young men of their own age and class, and discuss things and develop and change their minds and explore. This is the thing we're cutting out in this country.

Q. What about the young wives? Are they usually other students or are they—

A. There's a pretty good tendency in this country for people to marry within their same social-economic-educational group, so these are not the landladies' daughters that the traditional Oxford and Cambridge student occasionally married to his sorrow.

On the other hand, these young wives don't have much chance to study any further, and, if they marry before they finish college and the husband goes on to a professional career, the chance of their not belonging to the same educational level as their husbands by the time they are age thirty is pretty high.

Q. What happens if there are babies while they are still in college?

A. If there are babies, it means, you know, the father's term paper gets all mixed up with the baby's bottle. This was fine in the GI days when young fathers learned to enjoy their babies, and they lived in trailers with a baby and a doctor's dissertation and a bed arranged in a row within a very narrow space. The fathers got interested in their babies and began enjoying them. We now have a tremendous crop of young fathers who enjoy their babies, often more than their mothers do.

Babies are, in fact, very engrossing objects. They've engrossed women for hundreds of thousands of years, and it now looks as if they were going to engross men, too. And the question is, is anybody going to have time to pay attention to anything else?

Q. "Anything else" being the husband or the wife?

A. No, no. "Anything else" being sports, statesmanship, art, science, exploration of outer space. Those are a few of the other little things we're going to have to work on in the next quarter century.

Q. Should men be more concerned with those things than women?

A. They have been traditionally. In human society achievement has always been something that men did. It didn't make any difference what it was.

I've worked in societies where something you might call "dressing dolls" on rather an elegant scale is something that men do. But if it's something that men do, it's achievement. If it's something that women do, it isn't achievement. And one can relate this directly to the fact that women, after all, do have the task of producing the babies initially, giving more time and attention to them than the husbands do, and they are tremendously satisfied by it. Producing a whole human being is a very satisfactory thing to do.

Meanwhile, men have crossed rivers, built ocean liners, built airships, built empires and scientific systems and written great works. And now, if we're going to have both men and women devoting all their time to infants, it's a little problematic what's going to happen to the world.

Q. What kind of students are these married undergraduates?

A. Oh, I think on the whole they're good students in the sense that they get through their exams.

Q. They get good grades?

A. Well, they get passing grades. If they need scholarships, they work for the grades that are necessary for the scholarships, but they don't work for the subject matter any more—it's just that they've got to get through. They've got to get the next degree, so that they can get the next job or the next fellowship grant so that they can support their children.

So, they are hard-working, industrious students. But their role as students is somewhat tempered by the fact that so many of the boys have jobs. I don't want to leave the impression that only the girls are working—especially in the nonresidential colleges, the boys are working terribly hard. Many of them are carrying full-time jobs as subway guards and factory workers and taxi drivers and heaven knows what.

This means they often don't have any time to do any intellectual work. You find a trend to try to get everything that students need into paper books, for instance, so they can buy them cheaply and carry them around in their pocket if they can't get to a library. Everywhere you are finding these big bunches of readings, made up from articles from periodicals, because students are never going to get near a scientific journal or a literary journal. They simply don't have the time to get into the library.

Q. Do you think there will be lasting effects on the country, as a result?

A. Early student marriage is domesticating boys so early they don't have a chance for full intellectual development. They don't have a chance to give their entire time, not necessarily to study in the sense of staying in the library—though libraries are pretty well deserted today except in ivy-clad, one-sex colleges, or where the libraries are good dating spots—but in the sense that the married students don't have time to experiment, to think, to sit up all night in bull sessions, to develop as individuals.

This is not only important for the intellectuals, but also the boys who are going to be the future statesmen of the country and lawyers and doctors and all sorts of professional men; even men studying for the ministry don't have time to think about theology because they're busy going home to look after the baby.

There is a tendency to substitute easy domesticity for a period of stretching one's intellectual and ethical muscles before one settles down.

Q. How about the girl's intellectual development? Is a college marriage likely to have bad effects for her, in your opinion?

A. Yes, I think it's bad for women, too, because it's in high school and college that you learn to make friends, and making friends is as important for women as it is for men. It's as important in all the terms I've discussed for men—to find out what you think about, how your mind works, whether you can write poetry or not or whether you want to go out and run for the Senate. These are all things that one ought to thresh out with members of one's own sex at about the same age level.

Also, with our present differential death rate—and there doesn't seem to be any reason to hope that this will be stopped very quickly—not the way we're making young men take responsibility now—a great proportion of American women are going to outlive their husbands. They're going to live in a world as populated by women as a convent was once populated by women, and they had better learn to make friends with them before they get married or they're going to be very lonely afterwards or very useless.

Q. Are the student marriages lasting? Is a marriage at, say, age twenty-two or twenty-three, following graduation from college, more likely to be successful than a marriage in college?

A. I don't think we know. A great many of these early marriages—if they have children very early—sometimes seem to be surviving reasonably well, as far as the mere survival of the marriage is concerned.

The fathers, as I said before, enjoy their children very much, and take a lot of care of them. So that they may get caught in a kind of mutually happy nest-building which I don't think is very good for the country because it cuts us off from a lot of talent, but it is a perfectly contented setup for the nestlings.

Q. Is it really "perfectly contented" for the nestlings?

A. Many of these present-day marriages provide very good nests. Without children, however, these youthful marriages are becoming increasingly unstable. Students usually are too young to be permitted to adopt children, even though married. Yet we firmly believe that there is something wrong with a marriage without children. We don't permit anybody to elect childlessness today. We don't even permit them to say they'd rather not have children for five years. This is regarded as unnatural.

The result is that marriages without children—especially where the wife is supporting the husband—are probably one of our most unstable groups of marriage in the country.

So, we have a tremendous amount of broken marriages in this early age group.

Q. Is the fact that the college man is supported by his wife an added tie to the marriage—or an added strain?

A. I don't think it's a good thing at all, because I don't think any American young man really feels he's a man if he's supported by his wife. So, he lets her support him, turns her into his mother, whom he is more willing to have support him, and, when he gets whatever degree she's supporting him for—especially if there are no children—he's very likely to leave.

Q. Is that what happens?

A. That is what is said to be happening and I've tried it out on audiences all over the country, and the audiences agree that this is what's happening. We haven't any nation-wide statistics on the subject.

We even have colleges giving certificates to the wives for pushing their husbands through college. But how many men want to be married to women who pushed them through college—you know, there may be some, but it isn't exactly in line with our existing American cultural ideals. . . .

Q. What kind of future do you see for these student married couples?

A. Well, that is a question. The men will have cut short their careers and their professional training. They will have made a very large number of substantial sacrifices, both in their own growth and in what they could do for the community, because the two go together. And they will still be paying for a house which they couldn't afford and probably still can't afford, in which the wallpaper will be pretty well damaged, if there's any left on the wall.

Q. Isn't marriage on the installment plan, orthodontia on the installment plan, house buying on the installment plan—isn't that, in effect, planning?

A. Yes, it's planning all right, but it's not planning for goals, it's an immediate solution. I mean that is true for the people who buy extensively on the installment plan—everything on the installment plan. This is characteristically not a middle-class pattern. It is a pattern that started with the urban poor. The idea was: Suppose you did buy a very nice icebox or a sewing machine, and in three months you couldn't pay for it and they came and took it away? Well, you'd had it for three months.

This is the kind of attitude toward life which we used to associate with the exact opposite of planning. It still means psychologically that you do not anticipate what it's going to be like in those later years, after the children have left home, and there are still many years of life ahead.

Now, at the same time, we've got a good deal of material that suggests quite accurately to these young people—who have been very well counseled on the career side—what income they're going to make in any special kind of job in five years. When you ask them what they're going to earn, they say they're going to make $5,000 to $6,000 four years after getting out of college.

Q. Isn't $5,000 to $6,000 a year rather low?

A. Not for people whose parents were working-class people in the depression. It sounds like an enormous amount of money. But if you ask them what they're going to buy with it, and only ask for the objects—not for the price—they will state a standard of living that takes $30,000 to $35,000 a year. This is the picture that's being presented to them.

Q. Do these youngsters think that far ahead—to the house in the suburbs, two cars and other things?

A. If you discuss marriage and having children, the second car will be brought in, plus membership in a nice country club.

Q. Is that typical of the thinking among student married couples?

A. Once they're married, they plunge into the installment-buying world in many instances. We do have one group of young people who more or less maintain the class level of their parents, who are exceedingly realistic on the whole. You find them among the children of professional people who are going to be professional people themselves, among the members of the Junior League whose mothers were members of the Junior League. Their mothers had servants, and they have none. The daughters have a cleaning woman once a week. We have this whole group of very realistic budgeters among the young married group of people who aren't planning to change their social-educational level from that of their parents.

But many other people who are going to college, or who have graduated from college in recent years, had parents who did not go to college, and who lived in a different period on a very different socio-economic level. . . .

Q. How would you summarize what early marriage is doing to the nation?

A. If you have everybody settle down at the earliest possible moment, never experiment, never try a new job if they can help it but stick to the old one that's safe, never go on to more education because they're already saddled with children—you're going to get a settled, security-loving, unadventurous people, just at the moment in history when the people of countries like China, and India, and Soviet Russia—although that's getting to be rather an old country—feel that the future belongs to them, it's worth sacrificing for, it's worth working for.

If we just retire into a kind of fur-lined domesticity, in which everybody in the country is concerned only with his own little family and his own little house, I think it is going to curtail seriously the contribution that we can make as a nation to the development of civilization on this planet.

Q. Will that affect our own security, too?

A. Certainly, because our own security today depends entirely on our ability to participate effectively in the world scene.

Q. Quite frankly, do you regard these young marriages in general as a menace?

A. I think it's the pressure on young people to marry that is a menace. This is the way I'd like to say it, because otherwise it looks as if we were blaming the young people, and I'm not blaming the young people. They are responding to pressures, most of which they don't recognize.

MARRIED UNDERGRADUATES ON THE CAMPUS: AN APPRAISAL [2]

In the late 1940's a development of far-reaching consequence occurred in college and university education. The arrival of World War II veterans on campuses shattered almost overnight the tradition that an undergraduate college student body should be composed almost exclusively of unmarried students. Some of the veterans brought wives and children with them; others acquired them after their arrival. Students who were combining marriage and the pursuit of an education were found in practically every classroom.

Those concerned with higher education raised many questions about this development. Two common questions were:

[2] From article by Lester A. Kirkendall, professor, Department of Family Life, Oregon State University. *Family Life Coordinator*. 5:54-63. D. '56. Reprinted by permission of the E. C. Brown Trust of Portland, Oregon, publisher of the *Family Life Coordinator*.

1. Once the GI government-subsidized veteran group is graduated will campus marriage disappear?

2. Can marriage and securing an education (and often child rearing as well) be successfully combined? Can a family man or woman also do acceptable work as a student?

With time answers to these questions have emerged. We now know that campus marriages are here to stay. The presence of married students in a college does not depend entirely on financial subsidy from the government as some suggested. There are still married persons on most campuses who are receiving direct financial subsidy from the government, but they probably comprise a much smaller proportion of the total married student population than they did in the late 1940's. At the same time it is probable that on most campuses the proportion of the entire student body which is married has grown. . . .

Neither is there any longer any debate as to the possibility of completing a college education even though married. Too many persons have done it successfully to leave any doubt. Not all who have tried it have been successful, but so many have and have been so outstandingly successful that all doubts about the possibility of successfully combining marriage and a college education have disappeared.

Having settled these questions college faculties and administrators seemingly turned their attention to other problems. . . .

Many persons working with college students are increasingly concerned with what has become a pretty standard arrangement for couples in a campus marriage, namely, the practice of the wife working full-time to support the couple or the family financially while the husband continues his education. . . . This arrangement has enabled many a husband to finish school, but many wonder at what expense to the wife, the marriage, and the children, if there are any.

Under the above-mentioned arrangement, the wife forgoes her education for the purpose of putting her husband through school. After that she expects ordinarily to become a full-time homemaker. Most couples feel that this will be the most profitable arrangement for them in the long run. Yet, it may ignore the fact that in the modern professional and business world more and more families are living on a standard which demands two incomes rather than one. After the couple leave the campus the wife may wish to work. One needs to add to this the number of wives who at some later time must become self-supporting, and the number who will require some kind of out-of-the-household work for personal satisfaction after the children are in school or have reached adolescence. The size of this group makes it readily apparent that many families may be working against their long-time best interests by accepting an arrangement which deprives the wife of her opportunity to get an education.

Another problem arising from the arrangement in which the wife stops her education to work to put hubby through is that it may produce a vast chasm intellectually between husband and wife. A wife sometimes finds herself in a routine, dead-end job which may provide enough money for the husband to complete his college education, but which offers her no real opportunity for personal growth and development. At the same time the husband is pursuing an educational program which results in intellectual growth and the creation of interests which carry him beyond those of his wife. The educational gap between husband and wife is slowly and gradually increased. Sometimes at the end of the college educational program couples are already unhappily aware that the husband has outpaced his wife. They are in the sad plight of finding that the very sacrifices of the wife which made possible the husband's education have created a gulf between them and endangered their marriage. One wonders with how many other couples this same chasm shows up in later life, particularly in families where the business and professional success of the husband depends in part on the education, interests, and social competency of his wife.

The result mentioned above is not a necessary concomitant of the wife working while the husband goes to school. It is, however, a hazard of which a couple should be aware. Presumably it can be avoided by careful planning and the development of a sound companionship relationship between husband and wife.

Certain attitudes and practices in the college itself seem to encourage the pattern of wife-working-while-husband-goes-to-college. The encouragement may be overt or covert, but practices should be examined to note the underlying assumptions.

For example, the common plan of granting the wives of married students the honorary degree, P.H.T. (Pushed Hubby Through), is a generous and good-hearted gesture. But does it at the same time encourage and establish the pattern under question to the detriment of both husband and wife?

Early in the history of campus marriages it was feared that the reversal of roles might be a source of conflict. That possibility was anticipated in situations in which the wife assumed the more-or-less traditional masculine activities of the family, while the husband continued school and took over some of the traditional feminine activities. The earlier concern of onlookers centered around a fear that men and women might feel ill at ease and uncertain as they engaged in tasks which were normally those allotted to members of the other sex. There is little evidence that this pattern of role reversal has been a very serious matter. The experiences of couples indicate rather that it has been healthy. From it each partner learned something of the problems and difficulties which confront the other as he performs his respective part in the maintenance of family life through carrying out the daily routines.

We may need, however, to be concerned with this problem at a deeper level. Counselors sometimes work with students in marital difficulty whose trouble seems to arise from certain feelings about role reversal. For example, some working wives harbor a resentment over the feeling that their husbands seem to be taking their efforts too casually. Some wives have expressed doubts that their husbands really wanted to assume the responsibilities and obligations of the head of the family.

A counselor sometimes finds the husband feeling dissatisfied with his role. He feels he is "cutting a pretty poor picture" as a man. Traditionally, he has assumed that upon marriage he would become the income-producer and head of the family. He finds instead that his wife has taken over those functions, and even though she makes no attempt to take advantage of the situation, her role as income-producer puts her in a dominant position. The husband finds that the planning has to be centered about what the wife can do, and his activities are necessarily dependent upon hers because she is providing the income.

In a number of these situations it appears that the conflict can be solved only after the husband is out of school, has a job in his own right, and is able to assume the role he feels he rightfully ought to play. . . .

Another problem is that some couples, particularly those on very limited incomes, lead a more dreary and unrewarding existence than they ought to lead. This is particularly true when they have to, or do, forgo so many rich and valuable social and cultural opportunities simply to maintain a minimum standard of living. Some couples marry very early in their college career and thus miss most of the social, extracurricular, and group experiences available to the unmarried undergraduate. Others, because of limited resources, find themselves carrying a burden of study and outside work which drags them to a low level of performance in many phases of life, both mentally and physically. Some find little time to give to the development of their marital relationship. How many married students face such circumstances is impossible to say. But one has only to discuss their situation with those who are in such circumstances to know that often the burden is heavy, that they are unhappy, and that the level of study and work efficiency is low.

Other problems could be mentioned. It seems better, however, to consider them in relation to some recommendations about campus marriages.

1. Strong consideration should be given to arrangements for both husband and wife to continue their education. When it is necessary to work to get through college perhaps both should plan to work. This kind of arrangement means that there is less chance of role reversal of the damaging sort, and that the wives are not completely relinquishing their opportunities for securing an education. They have a better chance of growing and maturing along with their husbands. This is equally to the advantage of both. . . .

2. Marriage might better take place at the mid-point or later in the college career. If a couple enters marriage earlier than this they have a longer time in which financial scrimping will be necessary. Pregnancy is less likely to disrupt their plans. Sacrifices and hard work often strengthen a marriage, but continued and unrelieved strains can also weaken it. A couple might, therefore, be better advised to allot themselves a shorter time for enduring

such strains as will be necessary to put themselves through school when their financial resources are limited.

3. The couple might well consider taking a longer than usual amount of time to complete their college educations. Traditionally college education takes four years of campus time. Many couples are still seeking to complete their education in four years and at the same time carry a part- or a full-time job. They may get through college, but with a poorer quality education than is good. Or they may get through school, but at the expense of so much strain and tension upon them individually and upon their marriage that their relationship is damaged. Consideration should be given to various possible arrangements, e.g., full employment for both during the summer, a year's leave of absence from school to work, or year-round school attendance.

4. The couple might postpone the coming of children until the advent of children can be harmonized with the financial resources and the educational plans of the couple. This recommendation is less easily accomplished than some couples anticipate. . . . In one study made on the Michigan State College campus couples who had one or more children were interviewed to find whether they had planned for the child. The study indicated that a third of the parents had. Another third had not been planning for the child, but were not particularly disturbed over its advent. Another third had actually been seeking to avoid pregnancy for a time yet. In these circumstances many of the couples were disturbed over the arrival of a child before they were ready for it. . . .

5. The couple might explore the possibility of borrowing money to complete their college education particularly if they are within a year or two of graduation. Many couples are very unwilling to graduate from college with any kind of debt. Yet they may work so hard to avoid borrowing that this interferes with their getting as good quality an education as they ought to have. It would seem desirable for a couple to explore the ways and means, times and circumstances for using credit in order to improve, and if necessary, to prolong a college education which promises to put them in a good position as far as earning power is concerned. At the same time they may put less strain on their marriage.

6. The college authorities should reevaluate their policies and plans in relation to the needs and circumstances of the married as well as the unmarried group. The traditional college atmosphere which developed from years of dealing with unmarried undergraduates changes slowly. Some glaring absurdities occasionally come to light as when the failure or low achievement of married students is reported to the parents of the student rather than to the student himself. The same incongruity is found at the high school level when, after a girl's marriage, she and her mother are called in to plan her program, while the husband is ignored. Could any better practice for causing in-law trouble be devised? . . .

7. College authorities and married students both should study the possibilities which the college could offer married students for a rich positive marriage and family life on the campus.

College faculties and authorities have never or have only vaguely realized that the married group offered the college any unique opportunities or challenges, educationally speaking. They have simply been students, married it is true, but still students to be put through exactly the same mill as students in the old days when all were unmarried. The students themselves usually seem ready to accept this approach. At any rate they go along with it without protest. The few who sense a lack are merely uneasy, and without any concrete ideas about what might be done.

Married students themselves contribute to the problem. They often regard their marriage as really beginning after they graduate from college. Instead of utilizing available social and educational experiences or participating actively in college activities they live a kind of inanimate existence, suspended in time and space. They are working hard to get through school so the husband, or the husband and wife, may get into their professional activities, get settled in some community, and begin to live. When this occurs, however, they may easily find themselves in a community much more poverty stricken in its opportunities for their growth and development than the college community. They are likely also to find the responsibilities of beginning professional life very exacting. Having established a pattern of postponing "living" during college days they can easily go in for another period of relatively sterile existence while they are getting ready to "really begin living." This, of course, can easily go on and on.

For a campus married couple to assume when they wed that their marriage and family life has begun in earnest would seem far wiser. The patterns for living they develop early in marriage now are likely to stay with them. Suppose they held this suggested attitude and utilized the college environment as actively and as fully as they could. They might easily find their early marital campus experience had helped them to establish an excellent basis for stimulating companionship and interaction in later years of their married life. . . .

The college authorities might point to the many cultural, intellectual, and social opportunities which offer . . . special advantages to the young married couple. . . . On the campus they will meet other young men and women just beginning their family life and their professional careers in circumstances which will provide them opportunities to develop lifelong friendships.

The college campus, it might be noted, is an excellent environment in which to begin family rearing. Courses on child development and family relations can provide an important source of help to young couples who are having or are expecting to have children. Nursery schools and child care facilities can make it possible for young parents to have above-average facilities for the early care and education of their children, and opportunities for them to learn about the privileges and responsibilities of parenthood.

Parents, too, might be interested in seeing their children marry while in college realizing the value of this environment to a young couple. . . .

The college environment, broadly envisioned and properly planned, could provide rich and stimulating experiences for young married couples during the early years of their marriage and family life. It could challenge them and help them build patterns of companionship and stimulating interaction. These in turn could serve as an excellent foundation for continuing happiness in their marriage. It could afford colleges a real opportunity to influence the family life of an important segment of the population.

8. Careful study should be made of the problem of services for campus married couples. Among these are housing, child care facilities, health services . . . and family counseling.

MARRIAGE IN MODERN AMERICA [3]

American Marriage in Earlier Times

In earlier times in this country, for example in colonial days, the family exhibited more prominently than it does today what are termed its institutional aspects. Such elements as the support of the family by the husband-father, the maintenance of the home and the bearing and care of children by the wife-mother, mutual protection, the production of goods were considered criteria for evaluating the success or failure of marriage and family life. The man was accepted as being the head of the family. He had considerable authority over both his wife and their children. This authority was supported by the mores and to some extent by the law. There was a clear-cut division of labor by sex both in the home and in the occupational world outside the home. One could accurately speak of "men's work" and "women's work."

There were couples who developed deep conjugal love and devotion. But love, especially love with a romantic coloring, was not considered the *sine qua non* which it has approached today. . . . In their activities preceding and leading up to the wedding, young people had, of course, to get acquainted and to come into contact. But their contacts were restricted both by the mores and by the common practice and probably universal acceptance of chaperonage. There were at least some rules governing propriety relative to discussion, so that there were restrictions not only on the topics a young couple might discuss but also upon the content and extent of their discussion.

Undoubtedly young people made some appraisals of each other in terms of personal attractiveness and had romantic inclinations toward each other. There was a place for romantic love. But it was not allowed to overshadow other considerations.

[3] Reprinted by permission from *Marriage for Moderns,* by Henry A. Bowman, associate professor of sociology, University of Texas. Copyright, 1960. McGraw-Hill Book Company, Inc. New York. p 21-5.

Under such circumstances the answer to the question, "What are the qualities of a good husband or a good wife?" would reflect the emphasis upon the institutional aspects of family life. One might well imagine that many an American woman in the early days set up criteria not dissimilar to those expressed by a Boer woman who lived on the African frontier. Said she, "I am sick of all this talk of choosing and choosing. . . . If a man is healthy and does not drink, and has a good little handful of stock, and a good temper, and is a good Christian, what great difference can it make to a woman which man she takes? There is not so much difference between one man and another." Such an attitude makes choice of marriage partner relatively easy because the criteria of choice are readily observable and do not depend largely on personal taste. It therefore permits both more help in making the choice and more control of the choice on the part of the young couple's families.

In those early days many a couple considered their marriage to be successful in the absence of love. Because of this and also because of the widespread opposition to divorce and the division of labor which made husband and wife economically necessary to one another, the divorce rate was low.

To a considerable extent, education, religious worship, recreation, and manufacturing were carried on in or through the family. Because communities were small and travel to and communication with the outside were both slow and difficult, the pressure of primary group control was considerable. That is, the same group lived together, worked together, traded with one another, worshiped together, played together, banded together for mutual aid in time of crisis. Hence each family was an integral unit in a face-to-face society. This meant that, whatever the conditions and relationships within a marriage, the marriage was held together in part by forces exerted from the outside.

Changes in American Marriage

Present-day American marriage still entails an ample economic element and the institutional factors in family living are far from absent. There are still division of labor by sex, support, protection, and mutual aid, childbearing and rearing. There are still manufacturing activities, education of children, recreational pursuits, and religious worship carried on in the home or through the family. But the picture is changing. Many of these activities, at least to a considerable degree, increasingly center in nonfamily agencies. The increase in urban and suburban living has broken down the primary face-to-face groups, thus removing some of the societal support from marriage, not in the sense of reducing societal approval of marriage, but rather in the sense of there being fewer external, societal, institutional forces acting to hold marriages structurally intact. There is increased emphasis upon how persons of opposite sex feel about one another and what kind of relationships they establish. . . .

In marriage and in choosing for marriage, that element given greatest prominence is love.

Today in this country most people "marry for love," although physical appeal is an often undetected counterfeit. "Marrying for love" implies a primary emphasis upon emotion, upon how two individuals feel about one another, upon personal satisfaction, and a corresponding reduction in emphasis upon the institutional aspects of marriage. Hence, new criteria of success in marriage are established. New qualities desirable in a husband or wife are high-lighted. New opportunities are presented for richness of living and completeness of sharing in marriage. But along with those opportunities go new problems, for when people do not find in marriage the personal satisfaction that they anticipated, they feel justified in seeking escape. . . .

One of the side effects of "marrying for love" is an increase in marital instability and hence of divorce. This is not meant to imply that more marriages are unhappy today than in earlier times for there is no known way of making such a comparison.

When marriage is based upon love and when personal satisfaction is given more weight than institutional factors, the responsibility for wise choice of marriage partner rests squarely upon the shoulders of the individuals making the choice. Today they can and do get little help from their families. Often the help that is volunteered is rejected. In a way this makes choice of marriage partner more difficult than it used to be because the elements upon which it is based are less readily observable, depend upon personal taste rather than social standard, rest upon an appraisal of another personality largely extracted from the individual's background, and are so variable that each individual who makes such a choice assumes it to be entirely unique. One can hardly imagine an American of today saying anything even remotely approximating the statement of the Boer woman quoted earlier.

As contrasted with marriage of the past, present-day American marriage presents both sexes with a changed and expanded concept of the role expected of husband and wife. Put another way, each sex is expected to play a greater multiplicity of roles, to do a wider variety of things. In a sense, each individual is expected to be a larger number of different persons.

CHANGES IN THE ROLE OF WOMEN [4]

In the United States, generations, areas, classes, and ethnic and religious groups differ widely as to their previous patterns and their rates of change in women's roles within marriage, . . . [but] in general the direction of change is the same among all strata. There are no effective counter-movements, only varying degrees of opposition, hesitancy, and venturesomeness, toward development of a [new] wifehood and motherhood characterizable as yet only in the tentative terms . . . of a rudimentary prototype.

That such a consistent prototype appears to be emerging in America is a consequence of . . . powerful common influences, some of which are so comprehensive in their bearing upon social life that they shall only be listed:

1. The equalization of real family income, concurrently with its rapid rise, especially during the past half generation.
2. The thorough diffusion of favored cultural patterns, through restless internal migration and travel, almost universally enjoyed media of mass communication, and high levels of education.
3. An operative ideal of equality of opportunity, to which every minority or disadvantaged person can make public appeal.

Influences which bear more specifically upon the wifely role will be noted . . . [below].

[4] From "Changes in American Marriage Patterns and the Role of Women," article by Nelson N. Foote, sociologist specializing in consumer behavior research, Marketing Research Department, General Electric Company, and former director of the Family Study Center, University of Chicago. *Eugenics Quarterly.* 1:254-9. D. '54. Reprinted by permission.

Women of the educated and mostly salaried upper middle class are leaders, models and mentors in moving the public toward the [emerging] prototype. . . . This . . . accounts for their prominence in the analysis below. . . .

Decline in Economic Dependence

Legal disabilities of women were felled after World War I, but only World War II and full employment since have given them substantial movement into all jobs and toward equal pay for equal work. . . . Reports by the Women's Bureau of the United States Department of Labor show, among other marked shifts, 27 per cent of all wives in the labor force (1953). A wife's sense of economic dependence upon her husband is in severe decline, even if not working, when she feels she can work if she wishes, and at the cost of no severe decline in status or standard of living.

Married women were discriminated against during the depression; their sense of economic independence may thus depend upon continued full employment, but it may be more permanently structured. . . . Successive reductions of the normal work day and work week, . . . [together with the decrease] in time taken up by conducting a household, let many women enter the labor force who could not when job and home each were full-time [responsibilities]. . . .

Increased divorce rates in recent decades may partly demonstrate that wives can now leave their husbands with less fear of hardship. From the husband's viewpoint, this may make marriage more precarious, but to the wife it gives greater power to insist that the marriage be satisfactory. The decline of alimony awards may signify legal recognition of the availability of self-support.

Segregation of the sexes among types of employment and physically at work is diminishing, i.e., men and women are increasingly working together at the same jobs as well as similar pay. The equalization of social status [which this implies] constitutes an example to the community at large. Another function of coemployment is exposure of women to a wider range of potential marriage (and remarriage) partners, thus further reducing male advantage and strengthening the wife's position. Some husbands complain frankly to interviewers that working wives are hard to control, yet women . . . in the labor force [who have ever been married] have doubled since 1940.

More Financial Responsibility

Due mainly to the mounting kinds and degrees of wives' contributions to family income. . . [together with] increasing male confidence in their judgment, the earlier pattern of predominant male voice in expenditure is giving way to varied arrangements. Wifely participation in determining expenditures is less often through adoption of a rigid division of income and more through discussion and repeated readjustments. A substantial minority [of wives] handle all family accounts.

Among urban white-collar groups, wives contribute especially heavily to family income during the earliest years of marriage. Some married students are totally supported by wives while completing their educations, without embarrassment. Whether cause or effect of earlier marriage, parents of both are freer in aiding young couples. The traditional sentiment that the new husband must support his wife as her father did has attenuated in nearly all strata, in favor of a desire by wives to share in their husbands' upward financial struggles. The evidence . . . suggests that wifely income, while no longer conceived as pin money for purchasing extras and luxuries, has not, except in poor families, become yet quite as essential as the husband's. Being lower than his as a rule, it still tends to be conceived as supplementing and stabilizing his. Nevertheless, as already experienced by some couples, when her earning power comes close to his, its loss due to pregnancy can be quite destabilizing in the absence of a prudent schedule of saving and expenditure. Taking this into account makes the heaviest incidence of the baby boom among white-collar couples even more hard to explain but strengthens the expectation that these women may want to resume work, unless their husbands' incomes continue to rise rapidly.

Public recognition of the variability of these arrangements is found in the law which permits husband and wife to decide each year to file separate or joint income tax returns, and to claim appropriate allowances for dependents. . . .

More Sharing of Authority

Participation by wives in family decision-making extends beyond financial matters and is being enhanced by a variety of influences other than economic. Along with the easing of legal barriers to divorce, the sanction of public opinion against it as shameful has crumbled. Three fourths of the divorced soon remarry. As an ultimate defense against . . . [unchecked rule] by husbands, wider availability of divorce conditions all marriages. Whether it does so by causing mates to try less hard to master crises, or whether relationships are improved by the limitation of male authority, is unfortunately a much-debated issue as yet unsettled by research. Several studies . . . agree on a substantial inverse correlation between economic status and frequency of divorce, with professional groups—the most equalitarian—divorcing least.

Male pretensions to superior authority are widely ridiculed in contemporary comedy, cartoons, children's literature and other forms of popular art. . . . The common encouragement of adolescents to achieve independence tends to focus on fathers and tempers young adult male performance in turn. Masculine domination through greater physical strength, corporal punishment and open violence has diminished in even the most patriarchal strata, perhaps indirectly due to decline of occupations demanding arduous manual labor and the rise of those rewarding education and social skill. . . .

The role of the wife in sharing authority is concurrently being strengthened positively by her higher education, wider contact outside the home, the exercise of responsibility in civic associations, and explicit encouragement by "experts." The increased emotional intensity and psychological interdependence, . . . resulting from the small family's isolation from kin and parents, make the giving and withdrawing of affection a potent sanction of sharing. . . .

Less Division of Labor

A more or less pronounced differentiation between male and female tasks in the home has traditionally been regarded as a fundamental feature of family organization. But in those marriages among the urban, educated classes which have been taken as prototypical of change in all strata, there remain only two or three tasks securely monopolized by one sex, child-bearing and sewing by the wife, and the most arduous physical maintenance chores by the husband. Painting, repairing, fueling, car-washing, though still mainly performed by husbands, are increasingly undertaken by wives, often with their husbands, often alone. Wives in rural and lower classes have [in the past] often performed men's work, but more fortunate women have both avoided and been denied it. Such women are losing their inhibitions against it, . . . [and are also participating more] freely with men in physical play and sports. Sport clothing, in fact, is commonly the garb of suburban wives in such tasks, and their attitude corresponds.

On the side of the husband, the same crossing of ancient boundaries is fast becoming commonplace among the more culturally alert and servantless segments. Diaper-changing, dish-washing, cooking, cleaning, laundering, shopping—tend to become duties shared with the wife, especially when she works outside. Such sharing fluctuates, rotates and changes unevenly, frequently provoking conflict. . . . Thus American wives, between mechanization of the smaller home, factory-provided services, and husbandly assistance in their chores, are progressively relinquishing a traditional *raison d'être,* but are gaining greater companionship with their husbands and more freedom for leisure pursuits than they are fully prepared to utilize. Some resent this trend as somewhat an usurpation of their prerogatives, especially child-rearing, . . . but most welcome it.

More Companionship with Husband

Companionship is further advanced in play than in work, either inside or outside the home, [except] in declining family enterprises like farming and retailing. . . . The decline of segregated amusements and voluntary associations is pronounced, whereas formerly men monopolized political bodies [and] women cultural societies, and adult fraternities and sororities thrived. Coeducation has been a major influence in this trend, great state universities supplying a model.

It appears probable that the urban husband spends more hours per week in the company of his wife than in any decade since industrialism removed production from the home. It is becoming impolite to invite husbands only or wives only to most functions; and agreement upon friends and outside interests now appears as important in marital adjustments as [did formerly] approval by each other's . . . families.

In sixty years the median age of males at first marriage dropped from 26.1 to 22.6; of females, from 22.0 to 20.4. Earlier marriage, before the man has achieved financial independence, suggests growing companionship, but the decreasing gap in ages is still more indicative of the comradely relationship arising; this gap will probably decrease further, as will discrepancy in their educations. . . .

In terms of sex role and personality rather than sexuality, the extreme polarization of masculinity and feminity found in the past is diminishing somewhat as signified particularly in feminine sports dress and masculine beardlessness.

Recurrent Self-doubt

The rapid change of women's roles occurs unevenly amid conflicting conservative and progressive attitudes and is far from . . . [being] smooth and confident. . . . While the more backward undergo continued suppression, the same trends intermittently precipitate the more forward into mingled emotions of anxiety, guilt, futility, boredom, unimportance, resentment and regret over wasted capacities, punctuated by spasms of housework and "doing things for the family." Such a mixture of intangibles can hardly be captured systematically but has to be reported as a widespread characteristic of contemporary marriage. . . .

A major index is the efflorescence of many facilities for marriage counseling, psychiatry and advice seeking and giving. A perhaps more healthy response to uncertainty about how to encompass the roles of wife and mother, companion and producer, are the flourishing child study groups, family living courses, and popularized scientific publications presenting information and guidance to replace traditional prescriptions. On the most intellectual plane is the wide reading of a dozen postwar books, mostly by women, which delve rationally and exhaustively into their current dilemmas. . . .

Husbands, of course, have usually had their vocations from which to derive an unremitting sense of worth (save when embroiled in contests for prestige). But wives in large numbers have become disaffected from marital and familial roles which formerly engrossed them, without having fully arrived at a new self-conception which reconciles their competing aspirations. Until their destination becomes more clearly defined, it will remain difficult for their husbands or peers or the public to furnish the ratification that will quell their . . . [uneasiness].

THE NEW BURDENS OF MASCULINITY[5]

Interest and research in changes in men's social roles have been eclipsed by . . . concentration on the more spectacular developments and contradictions in feminine roles, and changes in masculine roles have been treated largely as a reaction and adjustment to the new status of women. Possibly one reason why masculine social roles have not been subjected to scrutiny is that such a concept has not clearly emerged. Men have stood for mankind, and their problems have been identified with the general human condition. It is a plausible hypothesis, however, that men, as well as women, suffer from the lack of a generally accepted, clearly defined pattern of behavior expected of them, and that their interpretation of the masculine role varies according to individual personality needs and social situations. The massive social changes initiated by the Industrial Revolution have not only affected the complementariness of the sexes but posed new problems of personality fulfillment for both men and women.

Analytically, contemporary masculine problems may be viewed as arising from three sources, which may prove difficult to disentangle. First, we may consider those burdens of masculinity which have survived from earlier periods, but which modern conditions may have aggravated. Men in their traditional role of breadwinners have always encountered difficulties, but it may be that recent developments in our occupational structure have added new tensions. Pertinent to this problem would be studies of occupational mobility and the increasing importance

[5] From article by Helen Mayer Hacker, lecturer, Department of Home and Family Life, Teachers College, Columbia University. *Marriage and Family Living*. 19:227-33. Ag. '57. Reprinted by permission.

of education as both barrier and base to economic success, of vocational adjustment and the new personality traits, such as skill in politicking, needed for high level positions. . . .

Secondly, it may be useful to distinguish conflicts engendered by feelings of inadequacy in fulfilling role expectations from those stemming from feelings of uncertainty, ambiguity, or confusion regarding role expectations. A man may have no doubts concerning the criteria of masculinity, but feel that he does not live up to them, or he may be unsure concerning the requirements for validating manhood. Preliminary interview materials reveal that the ideal man is considered by men as being, among other things, a good provider, the ultimate source of knowledge and authority, and strong in character so that he may give a feeling of security, not only financially but emotionally, to his wife and children, and it was evident from their further responses that the respondents found themselves deficient in meeting these demands.

The norms of masculinity, however (and, conversely, those of effeminacy) may vary among social groups, and multiple group participations may set up contradictions and inconsistencies in outlook. For example, it was only after several months of counseling that a skilled mechanic developed the courage to dust off some old Caruso records he had stored in the attic, and find that listening to them was no threat to his manhood. The group memberships of a professional man, however, would hardly produce this particular conflict.

The third source or way of examining the problematic aspects of masculine social roles is interpreting them in terms of accommodation to the new freedoms and responsibilities of women. Here . . . we may look with profit to the minority group literature. Horace R. Cayton has spoken of the guilt-hate-fear complex of whites in regard to Negroes. He says:

> Guilt, because his treatment of the American Negro is contrary to all of his higher impulses. . . . But having such guilt and being unable and unwilling to resolve it, persons learn to hate the object they feel guilty about so the guilt turns to hate and with it the necessity to rationalize and justify their behavior. Finally there is fear, for the white man in all of his arrogance knows that in spite of his rationalizations about racial inferiority he would be resentful and strike back if treated the way he treats Negroes. ["The Psychology of the Negro under Discrimination" in Arnold M. Rose, ed., *Race Prejudice and Discrimination.*]

Perhaps I would not press this analogy, if several men had not told me themselves that in their eyes men have guilt feelings about the whole history of male-female relationships, and that while the "emotionally stable" man was attempting to work out a new, more equitable pattern, neurotic men succumbed to the other elements in the complex by striving to stand firm on traditional male prerogatives or going too far in their subservience to women. Again, in the matter of social distance, some men are willing to admit their occasional need of exclusive male companionship, while others are afraid to recognize it. Some find friendship with women enjoyable, while others are as uneasy with "intellectual" women as the white Southerner with educated Negroes.

In fact the chief obstacle so far experienced in efforts to collect data as a basis for the formulation of precise hypotheses has been men's reticence . . . [resulting in part from] an element of the traditional masculine role which proscribes admission and expression of psychological problems, feelings, and general overt introspection, as summed up in the stereotype of the strong, silent man. True he may be permitted moments of weakness, some faltering in his self-appointed task, when he falls back on a woman for emotional support, but such support is in the nature of ego-building rather than direct participation and counsel. The ideal American male personality has been described by John Gillin [in *An Introduction to Sociology*] as a "red-blooded, gentlemanly, go-getter" and any confessions of doubts, uncertainties, or insecurities would tarnish this image, any sign of weakness might be taken for effeminacy. Perhaps this is the greatest burden of masculinity our culture imposes.

Nevertheless, there are objective indices that all is not well with men. Most obvious is the widespread expression of resentment toward women in conversation, plays, novels, and films. Modern women are portrayed as . . . Delilahs busily leveling men's individuality and invading the strongholds of masculinity in work, play, sex, and the home. She seems to say, with Ethel Merman, to the man, "Everything you can do I can do better.". . . In the comic strips, husbands and fathers are the guileless tools of their wives and daughters. To change Congreve's phrase in *The Way of the World,* many men seem to see themselves as dwindling into a husband or other female appendage. . . .

In seeking a conceptual model in which to cast masculine role problems, Kirkpatrick's discussion of cultural inconsistencies in marital roles may be of service [Clifford Kirkpatrick, *The Family as Process and Institution*]. He distinguished among . . . [several] roles provided in our society for the married woman, each role implying certain privileges and certain obligations, and suggested that conflict might arise from the disposition of the wife to claim the privileges of more than one role without accepting its corresponding obligations, or from the disposition of the husband to expect his wife to assume the duties of more than one role without receiving its corresponding rights. . . .

Let us try to apply this notion of ethical inconsistency to some of the main statuses which men occupy in our society.

As a man, men are now expected to demonstrate the manipulative skill in interpersonal relations formerly reserved for women under the headings of intuition, charm, tact, coquetry, womanly wiles, etc. They are asked to bring patience, understanding, gentleness to their human dealings. Yet with regard to women they must still be sturdy oaks. As I heard on the radio recently, a woman wants a man to be "big and strong, sensitive and tender, the sort of person on whom you can rely, and who leaves you free to manage things the way you want." This contradiction is also present in men's relationships with men. As [David] Riesman points out in *The Lonely Crowd*, now that the "softness of personnel" has been substituted for the "hardness of material" men must be free with the glad hand, they must impress others with their warmth and sincerity (rather than as formerly with their courage and honesty and industry), they must be trouble shooters on all fronts. Yet they are not thereby relieved of the necessity of achieving economic success or other signal accomplishment, nor are they permitted such catharses as weeping, fits of hysterics, and obvious displays of emotionalism. Of course, it may be objected that as women are increasingly allowed male privileges, they, too, are restricted in their emotional expression. Yet in the present era of transition women may still on the basis of the unpredictability of their sex, which is vaguely linked to biological functioning, have greater recourse to moodiness and irrationality.

In the status of husband, a man must assume the primary responsibility for the support of the home. A man who marries for money is exposed to more social opprobrium than a woman, and there is scanty social support for the expectation that the wife should shoulder half the financial burden. The self-respecting male has no choice but to work. . . . Yet his responsibility does not end there. Although he should excel his wife in "external creativity" he is also called upon to show some competence in "internal creativity" in developing the potentialities of the husband-wife relationship, and sharing the physical and policy-making burdens of maintaining the home. . . .

As a father, he bears the chief responsibility in law for the guardianship of the children, but often in practice plays a subordinate role. He may wistfully long for or stormily demand the respect of his children, but his protracted absence from the home makes it easy for them to evade his authority and guidance. Moreover, he is increasingly reproached for his delinquencies as a father. He is urged to strengthen his friendly, democratic relationship to his family without in any way lessening the primacy of his occupational role, though he is made to feel guilty for his efforts to support the home to the extent that they remove him from it. Indeed, the conflict between home and job is more salient and universal for men than for women. He has lost the security of the old *paterfamilias,* who was the autocrat of the breakfast table, and experiences difficulties in establishing a satisfying new role. That father is hard put to it to find his rightful place in the home is starkly summarized in the comment of the comic strip character, Penny, on the ambiguity of the father role, "We always try to make father feel he is a part of the family."

Father is no longer the chief mediator between the outside world and his family. As Gunnar Dybwad has said,

> While formerly the father carried prestige because he, largely, was the connecting link to community affairs, now radio and TV, women's clubs and school-organized activities have greatly lessened his importance in this respect. Moreover, with increasing mechanization, his maintenance concerns in everyday household affairs have decreased. ["Fathers Today: Neglected or Neglectful?," *Child Study,* 1952]

He may feel outnumbered in PTA organizations where mother is the parent most often represented. His absorption in work cuts him adrift from the new patterns of child development. It is mother who reads the child psychology books, accompanies the child to the guidance counselor, consults with teachers, and participates in community child projects.

Dr. Leo Bartemeier has pointed to a further conflict in the father role. In accordance with the cultural ideal of the he-man, fathers may feel that to be loving and gentle is consciously or unconsciously regarded as psychological failure, and indeed it may be difficult to make the transition from the attitude of ruggedness and toughness developed in schools, businesses, colleges, teams, and clubs to "the guiding light of paternal solicitude, love, and affection."

The requirements of the father role are further obscured by recent overemphasis on the mother-child relationship, especially in infancy. . . . Father is relegated to the role of mother-substitute or nursery assistant, and receives little help in becoming an effective member of the parent team.

As a son, he may face more obstacles to emotional maturity than a daughter. The dangers of "Momism" and the female conscience have been much propagandized. Exposed almost exclusively to the influence of women as mothers, teachers, and sisters the growing boy may identify goodness with femininity. Presumably the immediacy and comparative simplicity of the mother's role in the home is more readily grasped by the daughter, but the son finds difficulty in identifying with the largely absentee father and is cut off from his occupational role. His mother wants him to be an all-round boy and is fearful lest he be a sissy, but she cannot show him what it is to be masculine. This he must learn in the peer groups of the youth culture so strangely detached from the adult world. . . . The personality traits which are rewarded in childhood do not bring approval in the peer group, nor are the values of the latter always conducive to success in the adult world of college and business. Arnold Green in his much-quoted "The Middle-Class Male Child and Neurosis" [*American Sociological Review,* February 1946] shows how the blind obedience and "love" for his parents which brings surcease from anxiety and guilt are ineffective in competitive relationships outside the family in which independent and aggressive behavior is demanded. Integration of the conflicting roles of dependence and submission inside the home with self-assertiveness outside the home is difficult because of the guilt feelings aroused for either violating the initial submissive adjustment or for not making the effort to achieve. So the son may envy his sister's more protected role, because, although he is permitted greater freedom, more is expected of him in the way of achievement, responsibility, emotional control and autonomy. . . . Also to be mentioned is the greater social acceptability girls find in being tomboys than boys who incline to interests labeled feminine. One of my students reported that he wanted to skip rope as a child, and finally got social permission by saying he was practicing to be a prize-fighter. . . .

In general, it can be said that masculinity is more important to men than femininity is to women, and that sexual performance is more inextricably linked to feelings of masculine self-worth than even motherhood is to women. As stated previously, our cultural heritage has identified masculine with human, and both men and women aspire to masculine values. . . . If a man is not masculine, not a "real man," he is nothing. But a woman can be unfeminine, and still be a person. There is a neuter category for women, but not for men. . . .

By implication, if not directly, in the foregoing we have referred to men's occupational role, and we may now turn explicitly to this area. The problems which men, more than women, experience on the job have already been mentioned: (1) the greater compulsion to success, if not from themselves, then from their wives; (2) the lack of an alternative to gainful employment; (3) the identification of economic success with masculinity; . . . (4) the new need for politicking or using traditionally feminine forms of behavior for ingratiating superiors, customers, et cetera; and (5) the feeling of being threatened by women in industry, who are seen as limiting opportunities for men, diminishing the prestige of jobs formerly held only by men, and casting a cold eye on masculine pretensions to vocational superiority. Also to be mentioned, although not new and not confined to men, are the problems of obtaining recognition, usually phrased in terms of earning more money, and job satisfaction in the sense of feeling that one is making a vital contribution to society.

The presence of women in industry is a disturbing fact on several grounds. First, it is frequently felt that women are not gentlemen, that is, they compete unfairly by using sexual attractiveness and other tactics closed to or beneath men. If the distribution of the sexes in positions of power were more equitable, this objection would lose its basis. Secondly, women who have ample opportunities of observing men on the job are not so likely, in the words of Virginia Woolf, to reflect their image double life-size. The man's occupational role loses its mystery, and women need no longer depend on men as a link to the world outside the home. This problem, too, is one of transition, and should disappear when through habituation to working women both men and women no longer expect masculine superiority and establish casual, workaday relationships on the job. And if through propaganda and education the presence of women in the occupational world, like other minority groups, can be shown to raise levels of productivity and shorten working hours for men, then their competition will not be regarded differently from that presented by other men.

FINANCES AND ADJUSTMENT IN MARRIAGE [6]

Almost all married couples find it necessary to compromise and adjust in order to arrive at a good understanding on financial matters. Family discord is frequently attributable to a failure to agree on how to spend the money. . . .

Contrasting Economic Values

Why should spending money be a problem in marriage? Here it is necessary to look at the values that each partner has brought into the marriage. Our society places emphasis on money and material possessions, but there is no unanimity concerning what things are worth buying. Since most families do not have enough money for all the things that are desired, they must choose carefully in spending. This necessity for choice is the key to the difficulties that the husband and wife experience in the early years of marriage. They have come from families in which standards of value differ. . . .

For example, in a marriage the husband may be from a family where the available money was spent for good clothes, a good car, and frequent entertaining. With this background, his values

[6] From Judson T. and Mary G. Landis, *Building a Successful Marriage*, 3d ed. © 1958. Prentice-Hall, Inc., Englewood Cliffs, N.J. Reprinted by permission. p 441-53. J. T. Landis is professor of family sociology, University of California, Berkeley.

may center around making a good impression on neighbors and friends. The wife may come from a family where the chief values were getting an education, or saving for the future, or owning a home. During the courtship period the wife may have been charmed and impressed by the husband's free spending to entertain her. They ate at the best places, and she never had to wonder whether there would be a corsage when they were going to a dance. The fact that her family was more conservative in spending money for such things might mean that she enjoyed them all the more when provided by her fiancé. However, after marriage this same free spending by the husband may prove to be a source of friction. The wife may be conscious of the limitations of their income and may feel that they should be saving money for a home and for other things that are important according to her set of values. To her, the expensive pleasures they enjoyed during the courtship period can now be forgone in order to have money for things she considers of more permanent value. The husband, who has been accustomed to thinking of money as a means of providing pleasure and enjoyment, may not be in sympathy with what he looks on as a sacrifice of the present for the future. He may find it hard to understand the wife's seeming change of attitude after the marriage, since she appeared to appreciate his free spending during courtship. It would take some time for such a couple to get together on use of the income. Patterns of spending and value systems developed over a period of twenty years will be slow to change. In some marriages the partners will never reach complete agreement on the use of money.

During the courtship period a man may be proud of his fiancée because she is always beautifully dressed. He is pleased when his friends admire her appearance. After the wedding he may still wish to be proud of a well-dressed wife, but may find that his income is not sufficient to permit his wife to have the kind of clothes she has been accustomed to buying. The wife may feel that clothes are so important that she would gladly cut down on the food bill in order to enlarge the portion of the budget allocated for clothes. However, if the husband happens to be from a family that believed in "setting a good table," he will not take kindly to the idea of saving to spend on clothes. The wife will find it hard to understand how he can have "changed" so, for during courtship he seemed so proud of her appearance.

Some of such differences in viewpoint begin to show up long before a couple marries, if they are alert to observe signs of differences. . . . Many couples fail to face their attitudes openly and try to reach an understanding on such points during their courtship, especially if they are greatly attracted to each other and are being carried along by the sweep of their courtship.

Contrasts in Ways of Controlling Money

In some families the father takes all responsibility for spending the money, in others the mother; in other families the responsibility is about equally divided between the mother and father. Thus, contrasting family economic systems can be observed. The young man who comes from a family in which the father has taken all responsibility may be inclined after marriage to feel that he should control the money. The fact that his mother always asked his father for money when she wanted it seemed perfectly natural to him. If this young man should marry a girl from a family where the money had been controlled by the mother or controlled democratically by both parents, there is a good chance that misunderstandings may arise. This wife would feel humiliated if she were forced to ask her husband for money and to account to him for every expenditure. The husband might be unaware of her viewpoint and at a loss to understand why his wife should react emotionally to a financial arrangement that seemed reasonable to him. Such a couple faces the problem of harmonizing their ideas concerning the handling of money.

When couples differ greatly on how the money should be used, the feeling of frustrated irritation each may have sometimes affects their behavior in a variety of ways. The husband may become overly critical of the wife's actions in other matters. He may find it easier to be generally critical than to debate with her on the subject of economic values. He may engage in behavior she does not approve of, such as going out with the "boys" in the evening, or drinking too much. Or he may just become surly, moody, and hard to live with, behaving in general like a worried or irritable person. In many cases he will not have analyzed his own attitudes enough to realize why he behaves as he does.

Growing Together on Economic Values

Young married people often feel that it is conceding defeat to admit that they differ widely on economic values or anything else. Many couples in the early years of marriage try to keep up the pretense that they are in agreement on everything. In so doing, they make no progress toward harmonizing their ideas.

It is much better for the couple going into marriage to recognize that almost surely they will differ on some matters but to agree that they will discuss differences as they arise in order to arrive at working arrangements as early as possible in marriage. If differences in financial attitudes are extreme, it will take more time and greater effort on the part of both to reach a compromise.

The importance of talking things over in marriage, if couples are to avoid emotional explosions, cannot be too strongly emphasized. The time to talk things over is when any difference in viewpoint becomes evident, *before* the situation reaches the point where either one is ready to do battle. Some men go into marriage with the feeling that women know nothing about finances or that it is a sign of weakness for a man to need his wife's advice on money matters. Most modern women have been brought up to think that their opinions on money are worth considering. They feel that they should be consulted when important decisions are to be made in affairs that will affect their lives. Today relatively few women will gladly allow the man of the family to handle all money and make all decisions. It is more satisfactory for couples to talk matters over and share responsibility for decisions. . . .

Budgeting As a Source of Friction

Marital tension is sometimes increased through attempts to follow a budget. A couple may try to follow a theoretically perfect budget plan that may not fit their special situation. If they cannot make the budget work, it is easy to begin to blame each other for the failure. Conflict may also develop over failure of one spouse or the other to record expenses. Perhaps the husband happens to be the one who believes in keeping a budget, and his method includes keeping a record of every cent spent. If his wife is not good at remembering where and for what she spent the money, constant hostility may center around the budget. Such a wife may have no peace because the husband checks up on whether she has recorded her expenditures. A common complaint among young couples is that the spouse will not cooperate in keeping a budget. If following a budget becomes a source of friction, some other financial system should be adopted. Getting more for the family's money through budgeting is good, but if making the budget work can be accomplished only at the cost of peace, the budget should be abandoned or revised.

Some people who object to keeping records use the system of putting money that is to be used for different purposes in different envelopes. The theory is that when a fund is exhausted the expenditures stop. It is not necessary to point out the complications that may arise with that system also.

The budget should never be thought of as a means for one partner to force the other into line in the spending of money. If this attitude exists, something more fundamental is wrong in the relationships of the couple, and budget-keeping will not correct the difficulty. It will simply serve as a focus for their friction.

If a couple does agree on the method of budgeting that they will follow, neither one should become too concerned if the budget does not balance during a given month. Some couples enjoy managing their money to keep a balanced budget. They record expenses strictly and take pleasure in their success in living within the budget over a period of time.

Who Should Hold the Purse Strings

No set rule can be stated on who should have control of the spending in a family. One husband said, "My wife was a bank bookkeeper before our marriage—she is a grand family treasurer." He had been married for twenty-five years and was thankful that he had never had to worry about taking care of the family money. In many families it is more practicable for the wife to manage the money because she has more time to give to the money management or because she has better judgment about its use than the husband. It has been estimated that women do 80 per cent of the spending for the American family. The wife buys the food, clothing, and usually the household furnishings. These constitute the major expenditures for the average family. Since women do most of the spending, there is some logic in the belief that more wives should take over the handling of family finances. One study among young married couples showed that in one fifth of the couples, the wife handled almost all family finances. That system is probably more general among couples who have been married longer.

Many men appreciate having their wives take the responsibility for money management. Couples who have tried this system are usually enthusiastic about it. The wife plans her expenditures carefully when she knows just how much money there is and is responsible for making ends meet. . . .

In many families the responsibility is equally divided. The couple has a joint checking account and both use their judgment in the spending of the money. This system is sometimes hard to carry out smoothly in the early years of marriage. Only after people have lived together for some time and have reached agreement on financial planning and spending will they have enough confidence in each other's judgment so that they can handle the money together easily.

Some men feel they must handle the money in order to preserve their sense of importance and dominance in the family. A young man from a patriarchal type of family may feel that to turn over the money management to his wife would be to abdicate his place as head of the house. Perhaps the least desirable way of handling family finances is for the husband to have complete control. However, in many American families this is still the policy. In some cases it works satisfactorily, for some women prefer that their husbands take this responsibility. Some husbands attempt to use the allowance system as a means of control; this attempt may indicate that other adjustment failures are present in the marriage. In such marriages the husband may feel that although his wife dominates in many areas of family living, he can occasionally have the last word as long as he holds the purse strings. One woman, after twenty-three years of marriage, said, "I receive a weekly allowance that is sufficient for food only. I receive money for other things only after an argument." This woman's bitter resentment toward her husband extended into other areas of living, but the focal point of their adjustment failures was in their conflicts over family finance. . . .

In some homes the children are given a part in deciding how the income shall be used. This plan is especially desirable in the purchase of items such as a new luxury. However, small children should not be burdened with all the financial decisions faced by the average family. Financial worries are hard enough for adults, and little is to be accomplished by having children feel too much of the burden of financial responsibilities. As children grow older and have more understanding, they should be encouraged to take more part in money management in the family.

The fundamental thing is agreement. If a couple finds that one system does not work satisfactorily for them both, it is well to try another. Success is more probable if people can throw aside preconceived ideas and be adjustable. Money should smooth the path, not serve as a provoker of family battles.

HOW TO GET ALONG WITH ANY IN-LAW [7]

Live long enough and the chances are that sooner or later, one way or another, you will become involved with in-laws. Your whole existence—your very happiness—may be colored by how you and your relatives-by-marriage get along.

Because you've heard so much criticism of in-laws in general, you may dread contact with your own relatives-by-marriage. You may fear becoming an in-law yourself. By the time you acquire a mother-in-law, you may have developed powerful feelings about the whole species. For her part, a prospective mother-in-law, long before her children reach marrying age, has probably begun to realize what a difficult role she must play.

Are conflicts among in-laws really as widespread as they're made out to be? What causes them? What, if anything, can be done to prevent or eliminate them?

Although the answers can be important to your and your children's future, up to now no thorough study of in-law relationships has ever been made in the United States. Realizing the importance of filling the gap, some time ago I began to

[7] From article by Evelyn Millis Duvall, well-known family life educator. *Collier's*. 134:34-6+. O. 1, '54. The article was adapted from a chapter in Dr. Duvall's book *In-Laws: Pro and Con* (Association Press, 1954). Reprinted by permission.

collect data that might open up the field. So far, 5,020 men and women have told us how they feel about their in-laws and how they work out their relationships with them.

It will come as no surprise that many of these men and women reported troubles with their relatives-by-marriage, or that mothers-in-law, hands down, won the title of "most difficult." In fact, the major complaints against mothers-in-law formed so clear a pattern we can say that, just as certain diseases have a "syndrome" (a series of symptoms which together form a clinical picture of a disease), there is also a "mother-in-law syndrome."

It probably will surprise you, on the other hand, to learn that a substantial number of people reported no troubles at all with their in-laws. Some even were enthusiastic about the contribution good in-law relationships had made to their own lives. It may be that some of the people interviewed—especially older married folks not used to airing family problems—kept silent about in-law difficulties. But many openly decried in-law prejudice as a rootless myth. Their reasons might well be noted by the opposite school of thought.

Before I go into the details of our findings, however, let us consider for a moment the magnitude of the in-law relationship. Each year 3 to 5 million Americans marry. If we assume that both bride and groom have a mother, father and either sister or brother, each newlywed immediately acquires three close in-laws —plus a number of more distant relatives-by-marriage. Figuring with moderation, let's say that everyone who marries gets approximately six members of the spouse's family as in-laws. Then new in-law relationships established every year total 18 to 30 million—a considerable percentage of our total population. . . .

Our study . . . clearly has been in a field long deserving of investigation. It has covered people from every state, and from both cities and farms. Some have been married only a few weeks, others for forty years or more, but most for less than ten years. They were of many religious, ethnic, racial, national and socioeconomic groups. Some were interviewed individually, some in groups. Others we have analyzed through their written responses to a national radio network contest on Why I Think Mothers-in-Law Are Wonderful People. . . .

As our study progressed, three broad themes recurred again and again:

1. In-law relationships have changed as our patterns of living have changed.

Many in-law troubles may stem from the fact that young married couples today expect much more independence than their parents expected when first wed. In the old days, the bride got a dowry; sometimes the betrothed couple went on a "collecting party" to relatives' homes, amassing household equipment and farm machinery for their own new home; often newlyweds chose, without question, to live as an "extended family" under the same roof with one or the other set of parents.

Nowadays the dowry has been replaced by an education fitting the girl to share the economic burden of supporting her own household. Beyond a prenuptial shower and wedding gifts, young people expect little else to start housekeeping. Doubling up with either set of parents is frowned on. The couple who even briefly make their home with a parental family do so with the twin attitudes of "making the best of it" and "it's only for a while." As for a couple who have to take in one of their aging parents, it is considered deplorable that they must share their home even temporarily with an "outsider."

The generally held notion of an ideal family today is one that consists only of husband, wife and their children. There are, of course, plausible reasons for this notion. Most families now live in cities where living space is limited and household tasks few. Little space is available for extra people. But every system has its price, and the cost of maintaining the small independent family may be greater than we realize—at least in terms of the contributions in-laws otherwise could make to family life.

Take the baby sitter. What used to be done as a matter of course by a resident grandmother is now an economic contract with an outsider. Similarly, the Visiting Nurses Association assumes the care of the sick, a duty once undertaken by one of the women of the family. So, too, old people's homes, hospitals and housekeeping services have taken over other tasks once performed within the family.

2. Another basic cause of in-law conflict involves what we can call the "elemental triangle of married living."

A story which cropped up in our investigation illustrates the point. A young husband was stationed at the Great Lakes Naval Training Center; his wife was living with their children at her parents' home in Michigan. Neither found the separation easy. Each week he phoned to talk with her. One night she tearfully begged: "Try to find a place near you for the children and me. I can't stand this living with in-laws any more!" Touched and baffled, he asked: "What in-laws are you talking about? You're living with your own folks, aren't you?"

This was her poignant response: "Everybody's an in-law when you're married!"

She put her finger on a real sore spot. Once a man and woman marry, they are faced with the challenge of identifying themselves with each other. They must adjust to new loyalties in which they both come first in each other's eyes. The process necessarily involves breaking away from both sets of parents.

But old loyalties and responsibilities carry on. Husband and wife still are adult children of their respective parents, and they want to be part of the families they married into.

Threats to the Newlyweds' Independence

Thus every married couple belongs to three families—their own first, but also his and hers. Unless the cohesive force in the new family unit is stronger than that which ties either of the couple to the parental home, the new family is threatened. Because the married pair must be autonomous if their union is to be solid, they are especially sensitive to any conflicting force from either parental home. Literally anything a member of the bride's or groom's family does which imperils the independence of the newlyweds can be construed as an in-law difficulty.

Our in-laws have a peculiar relationship to us. They are members of the family, but they come into intimacy with us full-grown, without benefit of much previous acquaintance. We know little of what to expect of them, or they of us. We want to be accepted as a member of the in-law family, but at the same time we demand the right to be ourselves, make our own decisions, live our own lives. This fundamental conflict within us is lifelong, but it looms especially in early marriage adjustment, when we are involved in shifting our identifications and realigning our loyalties.

3. Still another basic type of in-law difficulty stems from early strains and stresses we have encountered within our own families.

Something in our family history, or our own early development, may, when carried over into marriage, make us vulnerable to certain types of in-law problems or prejudiced against in-laws generally. For example, both childish dependence upon parental approval and adolescent rebellion from parental influence are poor ingredients for marriage. Not until we are emotionally ready to establish our own home with neither a need to be dependent nor an urge to rebel blindly can we accept without difficulty help from either our parents or parents-in-law.

Those Who Know How to Accept Others

Children who have been encouraged to love and enjoy a wide variety of people outside their own family have what it takes to accept members of the spouse's family without fear or guilt that they are being disloyal to their own. They have learned to accept others, and so are prepared to marry into a second family and build a third. . . .

All in-laws are difficult at times. After we asked 1,337 men and women to indicate the in-law relationship that in their experience had proved the toughest, and then to report what had made these in-law contacts troublesome, no fewer than 2,611 separate complaints engulfed us!

Here are some of the findings in this part of our study:

1. The largest category of complaints revolved around in-law meddlesomeness, interference and domination. More than 20 per cent of all complaints were of this kind.

2. The next largest category of complaints went to the opposite pole of the in-law problem, involving the problem of being accepted as a member of the spouse's family. Relatives by marriage were criticized as indifferent, distant and thoughtless.

3. The women interviewed had many more complaints than the men—an indication that the husband's family is more troublesome to the wife than the wife's to the husband—and

female in-laws were criticized more frequently than male in-laws.

4. At the same time, more women than men interviewed were appreciative of in-laws. The fact, coupled with the previous finding, can be understood if you realize that females of the family, rather than males, are responsible for developing close interpersonal and intrafamily relationships.

5. After mother-in-law, the in-laws most often mentioned as troublesome were, in order: sister-in-law, brother-in-law and father-in-law.

6. The chief category of complaint against sister-in-law was that she meddles, interferes, gives unwanted advice. In this criticism, she ranked below mother-in-law but well ahead of other relatives by marriage. Part of this failing seems to stem from sister-in-law's inability to realize that her married brother is a grown man capable of handling his own affairs, and part from a continuation of the patterns of quibbling and bickering that started in the early rivalry of brother and sister. The next major category of complaint against sister-in-law was that she is cold, aloof and unfriendly. It was evident that women expect female relatives by marriage to welcome them into the family. More often than not, "sister-in-law" meant the husband's sister, and an elder one at that; the wife's sister was least often mentioned as a problem.

7. Brother-in-law is significantly less difficult than either sister-in-law or mother-in-law, and outranked father-in-law as a problem only slightly. When found fault with at all, he was mentioned equally often by men and women. The top complaint registered about him was that he is incompetent; next, that he is immature (childish, irresponsible, dependent); then, thoughtless, indifferent, self-righteous. In general, criticism fell in those areas where other relatives have to step in and take over responsibilities, financial and otherwise, that they feel he should be assuming.

8. Father-in-law figured only incidentally in the complaints about in-laws. He rarely attempts to rule his children's family, as was once customary; compared to mother-in-law, his influence is small indeed. He was criticized most often, in fact, for ineffectuality. He offends by default, by his failure to be the

kind of competent person his children-in-law can be proud to claim as their own. He is also seen to be old-fashioned, resistant to change, boastful and too talkative. . . . Father-in-law also accounts for more than a third of all complaints concerning "unconventionality"—drinking, gambling, carousing—although in all, this charge did not make up a large percentage of the complaints directed at him. It would be absorbing to pursue the question of which came first, the unconventionality or the alienation within the family.

9. Children-in-law criticize parents-in-law much more than vice versa—an indication that not only are older persons more culpable, but they are softer in their own criticisms. One complaint is that parents-in-law are "old-fashioned" in the sense of disagreeing about traditions, resisting change and being uncongenial. It is interesting that parents do not criticize their children as "new-fashioned." Rather, in complaining about the children's uncongeniality, parents-in-law seemed to wish that the younger generation would accept them, rather than label them "old-fashioned."

Now we come to mother-in-law, far and away the number one hazard among in-laws. . . .

Our analysis of the chief complaints against mothers-in-law showed that their dilemma is similar to that of the porcupine, which can relate itself to its own kind only by being very careful: too close, and the quills hurt; too far away, and there's no contact.

First on the list of criticisms leveled at mothers-in-law is that they are meddlesome; second, that they are possessive; third, that they nag. Together, meddlesomeness, possessiveness and nagging constitute the "mother-in-law syndrome." These three jointly account for more than half of all complaints about them. On the other hand, the next ranking criticism was the complaint of distance: "She ignores us, is indifferent, uninterested, not helpful, aloof, doesn't accept me/us, is not close, unsociable, not motherly, etc."

A Few More Unpleasant Traits

Less often mentioned criticisms are that the mothers-in-law are immature, old-fashioned, thoughtless, pampering, self-righteous, talkative, gossiping and jealous.

Some other findings about mothers-in-law:

Nine out of ten complaints came from women. These data do not support the popular notion that it is the man who professes the greater difficulty with his mother-in-law.

Younger women feel the mother-in-law problem more strongly than do older women.

Many people showed that they harbored resentment against their mother-in-law because she had opposed their courtship of her child—a strong hint of the need for initial acceptance and mutual trust if harmony is to reign.

Residents of the South, where family ties and sentiments remain most deeply entrenched, make fewer complaints against mothers-in-law than any other region.

Significant differences cropped up among various religious affiliations. The largest percentage of mother-in-law "most difficult" mentions came from the Jewish group; next, from the Protestant group; least, from the Roman Catholic group. Although these differences beg for further study, one interpretation, on the basis of the few facts we have, may be that Jewish people in America are going through a cultural transformation from an ultra-conservative to a more liberal, equalitarian family and personal life, while the persistence of strong traditions for family harmony in the Roman Catholic group makes for fewer expressed conflicts between the generations.

Part of the high percentage of votes mother-in-law gets for being the most difficult in-law may stem from the fact that in our society she can be, indeed is expected to be, criticized without censure. On the other hand, our study turns up evidence that the mother-in-law stereotype is being renounced. Many of the people interviewed declared that to picture her always as an ogre was not only untrue but unfair; that it put mother-in-law in an unfortunate light before she got a chance to prove herself a loving ally; that it produced unnecessary stresses and strains on a new marriage. . . .

Many married persons of both sexes said that merely anticipating mother-in-law trouble sometimes made for strains in their new family that otherwise might not have occurred. Many told of their surprise when their mother-in-law turned out to be a loyal friend and companion. These people are particularly incensed at the injustice of the typical mother-in-law barb. . . .

Repudiation of the mother-in-law myth through actual experience is clearly evident in many of the cases we studied. The reasons given were many and varied.

Half the men and women who volunteered opinions about their mother-in-law said that they like her because she is a mother in some real sense. Some women appreciate the fact that their mother-in-law taught them, as brides, the fundamentals of becoming a good wife and mother. A bride can often accept such training more comfortably from her mother-in-law than from her own mother; with her husband's mother, she starts out as a young adult and receives her respect as such. A wife's eagerness to please her husband leads her to her mother-in-law, who can advise her of his likes and dislikes. This relationship helps both women maintain prestige. In fact, there seems to arise a pleasant sense of conspiracy-of-women when bride and mother-in-law join forces in mutual concern for the welfare of the man whose love they share.

Both men and women interviewed recalled gratefully that their mother-in-law helped them out financially, nursed the family through illness, was right there when baby came, saw the wife through the husband's military service. Still others remarked that she "reared the fine person I married"; others, that "she is more than a mother to me, for my own mother failed me."

One out of every four men and women who had anything to say about their mother-in-law reported that they liked her "as a person"—a plain hint that if we are ever to lick the mother-in-law problem we must encourage middle-aged and older women to live lives of their own.

What about mothers-in-law themselves? How does it feel to be one? Obviously, it takes a lot of patience to fill the role successfully. It isn't easy to leave the role of mother, where one is loved and cherished, and become a mother-in-law, where one is apt to be avoided and criticized as an accepted custom of our culture. That many mothers-in-law can stand all the barbs against them without resentment or retaliation amazes those who contemplate the problem.

Proof that mothers-in-law usually face the stereotype with patience is that they have never developed a parade of son-in-law jokes or filled the popular mind with prejudices against daughters-in-law. Indeed, the most striking finding in this part of our study is that children-in-law are not often criticized. This remarkable record can hardly be due entirely to the spotless character of the children-in-law; it must be that the prejudiced parental eye overlooks many human faults. When mothers-in-law do complain, the two top-ranking criticisms of both sons- and daughters-in-law are that they are indifferent and thoughtless—reflecting the eagerness of mothers-in-law to be accepted by their children-in-law, be interested in them, and feel close to the family.

Everything She Does Is Wrong

Some mothers-in-law in our study revealed an "I-can't-win" attitude. A St. Louis woman thus summed up the mother-in-law's dilemma: "If she suggests her son's favorite recipe, she's domineering. If she buys her daughter a new dress, she's interfering. If she rocks her grandson, she's old-fashioned; if she doesn't, she's a square in baby-sitting circles. If she visits the newlyweds, she's a nosy pest; if she doesn't, she's strangely aloof. Men have braved terrific odds to explore the vast unknown. But nowhere has their courage ever surpassed that required of a mother-in-law." . . .

What can those of us who are . . . in-laws, or just about to be, do to get along with our relatives-by-marriage? Can we improve, if need be, relationships that have soured?

Fortunately the answer is yes, we can—even though no two families, no two in-law problems, are ever exactly alike.

First, some guiding principles:

1. The best way to improve your relationships with other people is to change your own way of thinking, feeling and behaving. If you try to make others over to your ways, you may run into a wall of resistance. But as soon as you look for what you yourself may do to adapt more skillfully to the realities of the situations and persons involved, you make progress. In other words, you will have more success with your in-laws as you learn how to become a better in-law yourself.

2. Avoid pinning any "labels" on in-laws. Don't expect members of the older generation to be "old-fashioned" just be-

cause of their age; this belief is not only misleading, but erects a barrier between younger and older relatives. And don't assume that a mother-in-law is "meddlesome" just because she is a mother-in-law. Recognize that in-laws are individuals, each with his or her own rights, privileges, responsibilities, problems, hopes, dreams, mistakes. Each is worth knowing for himself. The better you understand him, the more you will understand his behavior.

3. Always bear in mind that maturity is important for family harmony. Maturity is not achieved in a single bound, nor at any particular time of life, but its rewards are many. You find personal satisfaction in everyday living. You don't have to depend on others for fulfillment. You become the interesting person others enjoy being with. You are able to relate yourself pleasantly to others. This quality makes for good in-law relationships.

4. Don't worry if sometimes you can hardly stand being in the same family with your in-laws even if generally you love and appreciate them. Ambivalence is in the very nature of family life. Whom we love, we hate at times. In any close relationship there is occasionally the need for distance.

Hints for Harmonious Living

Now for some lesser, but still important, guidelines for getting along with your in-laws.

Before you marry:

If possible, choose a spouse of similar background to yours. Your ways of behaving are more understandable to each other's family because of all you have in common; your roles with each other are in harmony because you have similar ideas of what is appropriate.

Get acquainted with your new family in advance. As you visit your future in-laws' home, you absorb the atmosphere in which your spouse-to-be was reared; you gain some preliminary personal acceptance; you take the first important steps in getting to know your new relatives as persons rather than just "in-laws." Conventionally, the boy has the advantage of knowing the girl's family before marriage because he calls upon her during their courtship. The girl rarely has this opportunity. Many a bride is precipitated into an intimate relationship with her newly acquired family knowing little of what to expect of them save what her mate has told her. Small wonder that brides in our study generally expressed anxiety about not being accepted readily.

Don't elope. Elopements make both sets of parents feel left out, and the hurt rankles in future relationships. As a rule, marriages solemnized by weddings and blessed by both sets of parents turn out more successfully.

If you are a bride-to-be, draw your future mother-in-law into your wedding plans. Not to do so may cause this particularly delicate relationship to get off on the wrong foot. One wise girl who sensed this danger consulted her prospective mother-in-law on the wedding details step by step. She found her deeply touched by this thoughtfulness, and then and there had the basis for a sound mother-in-law relationship.

After you marry:

Refrain from telling mother-in-law jokes and discourage those who do.

Keep channels of communication open between you and your in-laws. Don't stifle your real feelings; air them, so that others may know how you really feel and can in turn express their own sentiments and attitudes. Don't fear arguments; often, the real issues and values can be aired in a good constructive argument more fully than in any other way.

Face the fact that family conflicts are inevitable. No two people see eye to eye about everything. Differences need not shatter the relationship if you regard them without alarm, guilt, sham or recrimination. People who take this view learn to resolve their conflicts in ways that protect the value of each individual.

Try not to use your in-laws as weapons per se in marital spats. In the heat of the moment, don't lash out at your wife by exclaiming: "You're just like your mother!" And don't angrily accuse your husband of being "no better than that no-good brother of yours."

Make decisions of family interest jointly. As the relatives concerned are consulted, each feels "in on" the decision and shares responsibility for it. People of every age and relationship are apt to be hurt when ignored in decisions that affect them.

The Hardest Situation of All

If you live with your in-laws:

Develop, together, a clear understanding of financial, household and other responsibilities.

Make some provision for protecting the personal property of each member of the family.

Respect each person's need for privacy—opening one's own mail, answering one's own telephone calls and so on.

Encourage each member of the household to develop his own talents and pursue his own interests in his own way. This means you, too.

Jointly plan for whole-family activities so that each member may share in deciding what's to be done and what part he or she will play in the affair.

Unify the expanded family sharing the household by celebrations and rituals that bring the family close together.

As disagreements arise, take time to hear the others out. Respond to their feelings as well as to the "sense" of the situation.

Be reasonable in what you expect of the others. Perfectionists are hard to live with in any family.

If you have mother-in-law trouble:

Encourage your mother-in-law to spend time and money on herself so that she may gain the self-confidence that comes with appearing well-groomed and attractive. When children have grown and a woman is left alone with her memories, it is easy for her to lose interest in life and in herself.

Help her keep up to date on happenings in the world outside. This is a time of her life when a radio or TV set of her own, reading, perhaps a current events course, can mean the difference between a dull, drab existence and vigorous aliveness.

Encourage her to pick up the formal education she left off in earlier years and find avenues for untouched abilities. Refresher courses help many a woman better adapt herself to the changing needs of her growing families. Training in special areas may rekindle old interests, develop creative hobbies, sharpen salable skills and broaden the base of her activities.

Applaud, don't deride, her volunteer activities in community and church groups.

Whenever she performs any service for you, give her the courtesy of simple gratitude sincerely expressed.

Return her hospitality. Too many children enjoy countless meals at the old homestead without ever proffering a return invitation.

Reassure her if illness strikes her and encourage her to follow medical advice to complete recovery. Older women often overreact to a malady out of fear of incapacity.

Help her get her financial house in order. She may, if she knows her married children are "back of her," feel encouraged to assume responsibility for her own affairs.

Recognize her role in the family continuity. Don't wave off her accounts of family trials and triumphs, her old family jokes and incidents. Retelling them gives her a sense of importance she badly needs, and it gives your own children a sense of family stability.

INTERFAITH MARRIAGE [8]

Nothing is more deeply imbedded in American tradition than the right of a person to choose his mate freely without outside interference. Yet young people often find that the exercise of this right raises difficult problems, particularly if they happen to fall in love with persons with different religious backgrounds from their own. . . .

Every marriage brings together persons from different families, ranks, classes, and other diverse traditional and cultural backgrounds. "Intermarriage" becomes a problem only when some element of difference is seriously disturbing to the marriage partners or to the groups to which they belong.

Before we consider the problem let us take a look at the marriage of one couple of different religious backgrounds.

Sally, a devout Roman Catholic girl, meets Jim, a less devout Lutheran young man. They have about the same levels of intelligence and education. Their home backgrounds are similar in many aspects but different in others. But the main difference is in their religion. Jim does not want to become a Roman

[8] From *If I Marry Outside My Religion,* pamphlet by Algernon D. Black, chairman, Ethics Department, Ethical Cultural Schools. (Public Affairs Pamphlet no 204) Public Affairs Committee. 22 E. 38th St. New York 16. '54. p 1-24. Reprinted by permission.

Catholic. Sally does not want him to be coerced into changing his faith. The priest states the conditions under which a Catholic may marry a non-Catholic. Because of the haste and tension and manner of the declaration of "the conditions and requirements," the two young people are upset and arrange a marriage ceremony by a justice of the peace. Within a short time the young wife becomes distressed over the fact that "this was not a real marriage." She attends her church, goes through Confession and Penance and Communion, and upon the husband's promise that the children will be brought up as Roman Catholics, the priest marries them.

But the matter does not rest there. Although their marriage has many of the elements of success, the differences over religion continue to crop up and to be a source of irritation. Jim's mother cannot reconcile herself to having her grandchildren raised as Catholics; and Jim himself, though living up to his agreement, finds the arrangement increasingly distasteful.

At first Jim tries to bottle up his irritation, but this leads to unpredictable emotional upsets. He finds himself quarreling with Sally over unimportant and irrelevant matters when what he is really upset about is her insistence that the children be sent to a Catholic school—or perhaps it is the fact that the only friends who come to the house any more are Catholics. Later, under the goading of Jim's mother, the religious issue is brought out in the open as a frequent source of contention until finally the marriage itself is torn by conflict.

This marriage undoubtedly could have been a happy one, as have thousands of others between partners of different faiths, if the partners had (1) understood what they had to reckon with; (2) staked out their common ground; and (3) worked to make the marriage a success.

This particular situation has been mentioned not to dissuade anyone from a marriage outside his or her religion, but rather to illustrate some of the obstacles that must be overcome in such a union. It was not the differing beliefs that caused the trouble. They rarely do. When a couple is in love, when what they hold in common is stronger than the divergence in belief, such differences usually can be overcome. But when, as in the above case, there is pressure from one or both of the families, the situation gets harder to deal with. If a minister or priest intervenes, it may be tangled still further. Friends or the social group also may cause trouble where husband and wife come from circles which vary sharply in views, habits, and attitudes. These are not insoluble problems, but you should consider them very carefully before marrying someone of a different denomination or religious faith. For unless you want to cut yourself off completely from your family, church, and friends, you will have to reckon with their influence as part of your future.

Why Interfaith Marriages Have Increased

Despite pressures from home, church, social groups, and society in general, more and more young people are taking mates of other religious affiliations. It is estimated that today one out of every five marriages unites young people of different religious beliefs and ancestries. There are a number of reasons for the increase in recent years. Among them are:

1. The increasing freedom of the individual to move about and to choose his own friends.
2. The concentration of populations in larger towns and urban communities so that the individual and the family meet many different kinds of persons, whereas in smaller and more isolated communities they met only their own kind.
3. The increased mobility of the individual through improved transportation and the increased number of contacts in neighborhood living, in industry, commerce and the professions, and in recreational and civic community activities.
4. The lessened use of the home as the center for recreational life and social contacts, and of the family circle as the setting in which the young establish their social contacts with the opposite sex.
5. The fact that within a given community there may be a scarcity of eligible and compatible young people of the same religious group or that, for a woman particularly, the only way to marry a man of improved social or economic status may be to go outside the traditional religious group.
6. The increased number of women working and earning, making it possible for them to meet more men of diverse backgrounds and to be less passive in the process of choosing a mate.

7. The lessening of discrimination and segregation in housing, education, and employment, making it possible for young people to meet and know one another in work and study and play and to break through the old patterns of separation and prejudice.

Changing Attitudes

These changing attitudes—partly the result of changed conditions—also have contributed:

1. Educational programs have stressed respect for differences, equality of rights regardless of color, creed or national origin.

2. Religious programs have stressed interfaith cooperation and the brotherhood of man.

3. The democratic ideal of a community, enriched by the unity and cooperative relations of human beings of diverse gifts and backgrounds, appeals to young people as the only sound basis for happiness and peace.

4. The bond between young people and the religion of their birth often has been weakened by the failure of the religious organization to meet the needs of the young.

5. Although the orthodox and authoritarian of all sects oppose and try to prevent intermarriage by preaching and indoctrination and penalties, they all permit it under certain conditions. Some of the more liberal religious sects appear to have few restrictions and are quite prepared to see their young people marry members of other faiths. Their ministers are quite ready to perform the ceremony, and the churches recognize it if it is performed by civil officers, or by clergy of other faiths. . . .

Are Religious Differences Always Hazardous?

There are no national statistics to show just how the chances of an interfaith marriage compare with those of a marriage between two persons from the same religious fellowship. . . .

Experience, however, does provide helpful guideposts. Such studies as have been made indicate that the more similar the background, interests, and beliefs, the more likely the success of the marriage. One study, covering a fairly small sample, indicates the rate of failure is somewhat higher in mixed marriages than in marriages between members of the same faith.

At first glance these figures seem fairly conclusive. But when examined closely, they are difficult to interpret. Is the failure of these marriages due to strong religious convictions and conflicts over religious issues? Or is it due to other factors—the adjustment of man and woman living together, different physical and emotional needs, personal habits, early training, differences of taste and values, attitudes toward decisions involving vocation, leisure time, friends, finances, relations to in-laws? Or is the failure due to external factors, the pressures of families and religious groups and the community as a whole? Is it possible that the opposition is so strong in many American communities that it affects employment or social contacts or educational opportunities till it strains the marriage bond to the breaking point?

Religious Conflict May Hide Real Problems

Feelings over religious differences may become intense enough to wreck a home. But usually no one factor can make or unmake a marriage. The strength of this bond depends upon a number of elements. Often the husband and wife give reasons for their marriage difficulties which are far from the heart of their trouble. Frequently, an issue over which there is much conflict and unhappiness is merely the combat area in which hostility is expressed. The true causes usually lie far below the surface. Thus religious differences may sometimes be thought to be the reason but much deeper currents of feeling are the real cause. This may be seen in the following case:

A lawyer marries his secretary. He is of Jewish and she of Protestant background. Neither is religious in any traditional sense. Both families are unhappy about the marriage. The Christian family rejects the Jewish son-in-law and their daughter. The Jewish family resists the marriage, but they finally accept it. They attend the wedding, help the couple set up their home, and are glad to welcome their new daughter and the grandchildren as their own. As the years pass and the children grow up, the pressures for membership in a Christian church and in the Jewish temple increase. It is a suburban community and the religious and social lines are sharp. Even though the Jewish lawyer has an overwhelming majority of non-Jewish clients, the great body of these have no social relationship with him or his wife. Their chief contact with their neighbors is in the Parent-Teacher Association at the school, in the Community Chest, and in the shops. The wife resents the rejection of her children, who are attractive, gifted, and popular in school, but labeled "Jews." Neither husband nor wife is informed concerning his or her own ancestral faith. Neither knows much about the faith of the other. The religious issue is never an occasion for conflict. Both partners agree that the children should be brought up with knowledge of the Jewish and Christian beliefs and should respect all faiths as equal.

But there are troubles in this marriage. Many acquaintances say that the troubles are due to the difference of religion, but the difficulty lies deeper. The husband comes from a family of great wealth, a family of professional people with a tradition of learning, liberalism, sophistication. The wife in this instance comes of a family of moderate means and from a fairly conservative, small-town community. She has not had much opportunity for higher education. Though she has been a good home manager, companion, and nurse, she feels inadequate intellectually. The husband has turned more and more to his practice and to his business and professional interests. As the children have reached adolescence and the independence of high school and college, the wife has felt more and more lost. Conflict has arisen.

Some will point to this family as a good example of successful mixture—while others will find here an example of the failure of religious intermarriage. In reality, the deeper questions are—why did this man, with his unusual combination of qualities, feel the need and desire to marry this girl of a background different not only religiously, but socially, financially, and culturally? Why has the community persisted in labeling and rejecting a woman of Christian ancestry as a "Jew"?

The chief obstacle to a successful religious intermarriage is psychological. Marriage is an adjustment. Even the most perfect marriage has its moments of difference and misunderstanding.

Religious issues also may be the occasion of conflict within a marriage of people of the same faith. . . .

When a man and woman are drawn to one another, select one another from among many, feel a physical attraction and a congeniality and an affection amounting to a deep hunger, there are many factors which determine whether this relation will be healthy, happy, and permanent. Common interests, some similarity in levels of intelligence, a sharing of basic values—these are more important in the long run than any particular difference on any particular day. When both partners are basically well adjusted people and love one another and share a common concern for the same values, there is a strong likelihood that they will be able to work out their problems.

Yet when this is said, it cannot be denied that a marriage concerns more than the husband and wife. The marriage involves the lives and relationships with the families and the religious communities in which the husband and wife had their origin and childhood associations. Although families, churches and communities have only an indirect influence, they can do much either to complicate and injure or to support and further the happiness of those concerned. Thus young people who contemplate a religious intermarriage should be fully aware of the pressures that may be brought on them.

The Roman Catholic Position

The Roman Catholic Church today bases its position on marriage between Catholics and non-Catholics upon the practices of the early Church. Union with one who had not been baptized or who was an infidel was deemed degrading to the holy character of matrimony. . . .

From the twelfth century on, all marriages between Christians and infidels were null and void unless a special dispensation was obtained from ecclesiastical authority. Although marriages with heretics were opposed, it was not until the Protestant Reformation of the sixteenth century that the Catholic Church declared them invalid. But during the last four centuries, the Catholic Church has found it increasingly difficult to enforce its strict decrees on this matter. More and more concessions have been made for mixed marriages but always with care to guard the essential principles upon which the Church based her objections.

The Roman Catholic Church is consistent in its philosophy and practice. It does not consider itself bigoted or prejudiced in matters of mixed marriages. As one cleric has put the matter, it merely holds that

> the Roman Catholic Church is the one true Church. There is no such thing as equality of religions from the Catholic standpoint. Therefore, to have offspring reared in another faith is a catastrophe, since it denies to the persons for whom one has the greatest love the Grace of the sacraments and the solaces of Roman Catholicism in life and death. It means that one permits his children to be reared in religious error. Such words may appear harsh to non-Catholics, but Truth is objective. —No non-Catholic is compelled to marry a Catholic, but if one wishes to do so, he does it knowing very well what responsibilities such a marriage places upon him. [John J. Kane, *Marriage and the Family.*]

From this position, it follows, in the thinking of Roman Catholic writers and teachers, that the chances of successful marriage are decreased where lines of religious faith are crossed; that a Catholic comes into serious conflict with a non-Catholic partner. . . .

[Differences may develop on] such issues as whether to send children to parochial or public school, which Bible to use in the home, and what kinds of prayers, the extent of church attendance, the amount of money contributions, the practice of birth control, association with Catholic and non-Catholic friends, and the often conflicting interpretations of events in the contemporary world. . . .

The marriage of a Catholic and non-Catholic can take place when performed by a Catholic priest in the presence of at least two witnesses. If performed by non-Catholic clergy, the marriage is not recognized and the Catholic party is excommunicated.

When the Catholic priest performs the marriage sacrament, the ceremony can be held in the church before the altar only if both parties are Catholics, i.e. if the non-Catholic has become a convert, or, in rare cases, if special dispensation has been granted.

If the priest performs the ceremony between a Catholic and a non-Catholic who persists in his own faith, . . . the conditions which are required for such a union are: (1) that the Catholic will be permitted and assured free exercise of his religion; (2) that all children born of the union, both boys and girls, will be brought up as Catholics; (3) that there will be no other form of marriage ceremony before or after; (4) that there will be obedience to the law of the Church in the prohibition of birth control and sterilization and divorce; (5) that the Catholic promises to do "all that is possible to convert the non-Catholic."

Although the obligation to fulfill the agreement is a moral rather than a legal one, neither the non-Catholic nor the Catholic could possibly take it lightly. No marriage should begin with an act which involves dishonesty. The non-Catholic would be guilty of lack of integrity and would doubtless fall in the estimation of his partner. Insincerity on the part of either party in signing the agreement might well become the occasion for intense conflict and misery. . . .

Protestant Positions

Many other religious groups have also sought to discourage marriages outside their own fold. . . . Some Protestant parents and teachers and clergy even oppose marriage with members of Protestant denominations other than their own. They point out that agreement on basic religious matters is crucial to a healthy, happy, and spiritually effective marriage. Where man and woman differ on religious beliefs and values they actually are differing on a way of life.

There are also Protestant leaders who are tolerant and ready to cross denominational and sectarian lines. But most Protestant denominations today take the position that to marry a Roman Catholic is to risk contentment and success. Several Protestant denominations have taken a strong position not so much against religious intermarriage in general but rather against mixed marriages with Roman Catholics. . . .

In 1950 the Ministerium of Pennsylvania memorialized the United Lutheran Church in America "to formulate and declare a church policy and pastoral procedures with reference to the problem of mixed marriages."

Similarly, in 1948 the General Convention of the Protestant Episcopal Church, meeting in San Francisco, unanimously adopted a resolution patterned after that adopted by the last

Lambeth Conference [of Anglican, i.e. Episcopal, bishops, held in London]:

> Resolved, that this convention earnestly warns members of our Church against contracting marriages with Roman Catholics under conditions imposed by modern Roman Catholic canon law, especially as these conditions involve a promise to have their children brought up under a religious system which they cannot themselves accept; and further, because the religious education and spiritual training of their children by word and example is a paramount duty of parents and should never be neglected nor left entirely to others, we assert that in no circumstances should a member of this Church give any understanding as a condition of marriage, that the children should be brought up in the practice of another communion.

The Southern Baptist Convention and the International Convention of the Disciples of Christ adopted similar statements in 1950 and 1951 respectively.

No Binding Rules

Despite these indications of opposition to mixed marriages and to marriages with devout Catholics in particular, the Protestant churches generally have no regulations or rules binding their members or their clergy in regard to mixed marriages. Nor is there any legal consequence for a member who marries outside his church. The chief concern is to educate and counsel their young people concerning the difficulties they are likely to encounter in order that they make their own decisions wisely. Parents and clergy who are more orthodox in belief and more devout in practice are likely to be more fervent in their opposition to intermarriage.

Jewish-Christian Intermarriage

As with Protestantism, there is no organized, world-wide, disciplined Jewish hierarchy with authority to declare Jewish doctrine and ritual and morality, and there is a wide range of difference in belief and practice among Jews. Nevertheless, disapproval of marriages with non-Jews is fairly widespread. For the orthodox religious Jews, marriage is considered an integral part of the maintenance of the faith of Judaism: in the home the teachings of the Bible, holy days, specific dietary laws, etc., must be constantly observed. Loyalty to God, to Israel and to Torah requires marriage within the faith. And even among those who come from the liberal Jewish tradition with a minimum of emphasis on doctrine and ritual and custom, there is usually an acute reaction in the family and among friends and in the Jewish community to marriage with a non-Jew.

Just as with some Christian families, there may be intense opposition to the marriage, a refusal to attend the wedding, and even the extreme act of disinheriting and disowning the offending son or daughter. So also among Jews there may be social ostracism by friends and community. In part this is an effort to guard the religious tradition and perpetuate the faith. Even more likely is it that the Jews, no matter what the degree of religious devotion, are concerned with survival. For the religion of Judaism has been a crucial factor in the survival of the Jews.

Because of the age-old and world-wide prejudice and persecution of the Jews, the gentile who marries a Jew may find himself the target of anti-Semitism. Indeed, so long as anti-Semitism persists on this earth, the non-Jewish partner and the partially Jewish offspring may be regarded as Jews and must be prepared to develop sufficient security, strength, and faith to withstand this. It is especially important that the non-Jewish member understand the history and causes of anti-Semitism.

The non-Jewish partner must be prepared also for a certain amount of rejection by the Christian community and must be able to undergo this experience without becoming unduly sensitive or developing an overcompensatory defensiveness. Both parents will have special responsibilities to assure the children of such a mixed marriage a deep security in their married and parental love. Both will have to prepare the children for an understanding of both Jewish and Christian traditions and the possibility of anti-Semitic prejudice. Both will have to find ways to help their children arrive at a religious outlook in which righteousness and love become the common ground which transcend and unite Jew and Christian.

Both the Jewish and the non-Jewish partners to a mixed marriage may have problems in relation to their families and friends. Both may be rejected by their own people for leaving the fold. Both may be rejected by the family they marry into. Indeed, it takes great patience and understanding and persistent devotion, to break down the prejudices and to reach the hearts and minds of those who oppose the marriage of the son or daughter to someone of another faith or religious ancestry. Both partners may find that they have to seek new friends and create a community of individuals and families in which their marriage is accepted. They may have to go beyond the narrow confines of both Christian and Jewish communities if these shut them out. In the large urban and metropolitan centers this is easier than in smaller, more homogeneous communities. . . .

Families

The parents of the young people usually desire their children to hold their own basic outlook and faith and to marry those of like viewpoint and raise families within the fold. When questioned concerning the marriage of their sons, one study found that 20 per cent of the fathers approved and 80 per cent of the fathers disapproved selection of a mate from another faith. The mothers revealed the same attitudes, 19 per cent approving and 81 per cent disapproving. In the marriage of daughters, 14 per cent of the fathers approved and 86 per cent disapproved; of the mothers, 15 per cent approved and 85 per cent disapproved.

In fact, many parents find it difficult to accept and approve whatever partners their young sons and daughters choose. This is natural and human. But it may be a cause for grave unhappiness as in the following case:

The daughter in a Jewish family returns from college at the end of her freshman year and announces that she has "found her man." The young man is of Lutheran tradition. The girl's father argues that he has no prejudice against Lutherans. He objects to so important a decision while she is only eighteen years old and while she is still far from finishing her college course. He argues that she has had far too little experience for a wise choice. The father pleads with the daughter to wait, take her time, think it over. The young people elope and marry. The girl's father is distraught. He insists that he has no objection to marriage with a member of another religion or tradition; he feels bitter that his daughter made a crucial life decision on the basis of the irrational and emotional needs of the moment.

Deeper than the reasons given is the fact that the young man in question has had little ambition for an education, lacks the kind of energetic and dynamic drive which might assure a successful business or professional career. The father has always pictured his daughter's marriage as a union with someone of his own intellectual and vocational and financial achievements.

To many people this is an example of the failure of marriage between Jews and Christians. To those who observe more discriminately, it is evident that the issue is not religious but concerns, first, the preferences of parents in such matters as type of personality, intellectual and cultural levels, educational and vocational and financial considerations, and second, the haste, if not defiance, with which the daughter entered the marriage.

It is understandable, too, that where young people have grown up in a generous and loving home, they should want not to hurt their parents but rather to please them and make them happy. It is important, however, that young people make their own choices and that they make their own marriage and family decisions after marriage. It is more difficult for some parents than others to learn to respect the personalities of their children and their freedom to make their own choices. And in learning to make their crucial life decisions many young people can well profit from the counsel and experience and perspective of older people. But it is hard to accept the advice of those who are close and who are emotionally involved.

For this reason, talking one's marriage problems over with a teacher or social worker, a friend, marriage counselor, or clergyman is important. Young people are often in revolt against certain elements in their background or experience which distort their perspective. They cannot easily see the kinds of experience they may encounter in the future, even though these experiences may test their relationship to the breaking point. . . .

Where parents have kept a child close or dependent in earlier years, a mixed marriage may be hazardous unless the young person has made considerable progress in learning to stand on his own feet and is ready to make basic decisions with his mate.

Where the feelings of the parents on religion are intense and dogmatic, it is important that the young person know his own mind and take the responsibility that is his regarding his own life. In matters of religion as well as in other matters, a husband and wife should stand by one another and give one another security and backing when it comes to conflict with in-laws. . . .

Children

Children present the greatest challenge to those who enter mixed marriages. The problem is a real one. It has two major aspects which must be carefully considered by those who contemplate religious intermarriage.

First, the psychological welfare of a child, his emotional and mental health, are fundamentally dependent upon the security of the home, the strength of the marriage, and the ways in which the parents work together for the child's welfare. Religious differences need not be a problem. In fact, they may even enrich a home if they add to its security and strengthen the common spiritual values for which it stands. For it is not really the religious differences themselves but the way the husband and wife, the mother and father, see their differences that matters. Whether beliefs are the same or different, the kind of religion which means living in understanding and love helps create a climate in the home which makes for emotional and mental health. If, however, the parents are in conflict over religion, or feel guilty at having married outside their faith, the religious factor can play havoc with the welfare of the children.

Second, the religious training of the children can become ground for conflict and division. This is no simple matter unless both parents eventually embrace the same faith. It may afford little trouble if both partners agree to a broad and liberal interfaith training which might include the history of religions and stress an attitude of reverence, the worth of the individual, and the supreme importance of moral values which are common to all faiths. . . .

Whatever the difficulties, the married pair can work them out only if they themselves are sound in their marriage relationship. And they will find the task much easier if they have a common ground in belief and practices and have developed their own family rituals to bind them more closely together.

When a marriage is childless and the couple desire children through adoption, great care has to be exercised in approaching adoption agencies. In many communities children are available for foster care and adoption only if the children are placed with families of the same religion as that of the natural mother of the child. Where the law requires this, or where the practice of child placement agencies is sectarian placement, the couple of mixed religious background find it extremely difficult to obtain a child. Fortunately a few agencies put their chief emphasis on whether the couple are happily married, love children, have a good home, and would make excellent parents. . . .

Differences in religious affiliation and belief may or may not affect the happiness of a marriage. As with other differences, much depends on how important they are in the minds of the married pair. Where these interests are not very strong or where the couple are united in a basic religious outlook or where their love is stronger than traditional loyalties, then differences in belief or affiliation need not cause serious difficulty.

Religious intermarriage can be a mistake if the sectarian aspects of religious beliefs of the husband and wife are stronger than their love. These forces can pull that love apart.

If one member is devoutly religious and the other is weak in religious interest or nonreligious, and if the devout member holds a strongly dogmatic faith, it is difficult to see how the marriage can avoid conflict. Even if the nonreligious person is willing to yield on all matters, it is difficult to see how there can be a sound basis for growing love and unity. For one partner would be trying to bring the other to acceptance and outward conformity—that is trying to impose religion because it is so important to him. The other is accepting that imposition because it seems unimportant. Only a very strong love and many common interests could give stability to such a marriage.

If there are important religious differences, a couple should have other strong bonds to make their marriage effective and happy. There would have to be a security in one another far beyond legal obligation. There would have to be a strong bond of love, genuine concern for one another, and many common interests. Beyond these, each would have to be secure in his own faith and know the other's faith and genuinely respect it.

In such a marriage there could be no secret thought that "Thank God, I was born in my faith and not in his. Though I may say that all faiths are equal, I know in my heart of hearts that they aren't. I shall pray for him and convert him and save him despite himself." The difficulty in such a case is that the more one partner holds his own faith to be the one true faith, the less he can genuinely respect his partner's faith. And unless there is this recognition of the truth and value in the other's faith, how can there be equality in the relation of husband and wife? Or a sound basis for the rearing and religious training of children? Indeed, not only must there be an equality of faiths, but also there must be, before marriage, a thorough discussion and meeting of minds and hearts on such matters as religious observance, dietary rules, money contributions, the religious education of children, and the role of the religious ideas of families and clergy.

Only by knowing one another thoroughly before marriage, only by testing one another's values and seeing each other's religious life as it works out in the families of both partners, can there be enough knowledge to give assurance that religious differences will not break the marriage. It may be possible to make adjustment through discussion and compromises. But it is better to know beforehand what the real difficulties are and withdraw from the marriage venture, if need be, than to enter romantically a relationship which may bring only misery and conflict in the end.

IV. PRESENT TRENDS

EDITOR'S INTRODUCTION

The young person today enjoys a freedom of choice and expression that would have been denied him thirty years ago, but he is handicapped by having fewer distinct adult standards and models to emulate. He is led to depend on his peers for direction and the isolated teen-age culture which results often assumes the aspect of a "teen-age tyranny," as Grace and Fred M. Hechinger point out in the first article.

"Where is the College Generation Headed?," the next selection, is also somewhat critical of youth. Basing his observations on a tour of colleges made about four years ago, sociologist David Riesman concludes that many students perceive their schools and, later, the organizations for which they work as environments which they are powerless to change or improve in any significant way. Riesman questions the truth of this perception and deplores the cynicism, indifference, and withdrawal to private life which he found prevalent among young adults.

In the past year or two, however, Riesman and other observers have noted a revival of interest in public issues on the campus. Generally credited with spurring this renaissance of youthful involvement in social and political affairs are the Negro students of the South, who by their nonviolent, determined suit for equal rights, as exemplified by the sit-ins, have won significant advances for their people. In "Strategy of a Sit-in," Professor C. Eric Lincoln of Clark College in Atlanta acquaints the reader with the details of how one series of sit-ins in Atlanta was organized and carried out.

Thomas Hayden, a recent University of Michigan graduate and a participant in the liberal student movement, describes in the next article how conservative and liberal student organizations have acted in politics and on issues like ROTC, disarmament, and the desirability of the House Committee on Un-American Activities (HUAC).

Perhaps the most compelling call to public service for the young has been sounded by the Peace Corps, which offers them a unique opportunity to contribute personally to the improvement of underdeveloped nations. President Kennedy's message to Congress, asking for the establishment of a permanent corps, outlines his view of the functions and organization of this body. "An ABC of the Peace Corps" and "Peace Corps Finds It Is in Demand," accounts from the New York *Times*, supply more specific details and bring the record of achievements up to date. And finally, "A Force of Youth as a Force for Peace" describes Crossroads Africa—one of the many projects sponsored by private organizations, in which students had participated abroad even before the advent of the Peace Corps idea.

TEEN-AGE TYRANNY EXTENDS ITS EMPIRE [1]

A recent newspaper advertisement, offering "teen-age charge accounts," emphatically made the point that no adult signatures were required. "Pick it out. Take it with you," the ad told its young readers.

This is only one of many manifestations of a growing and unreasonable domination by teen-agers over American adults, American life and American standards.

The teen-age tyranny is partly the result of adult abdication of responsibility. It is also the natural consequence of widespread misinterpretation by parents and teachers of the meaning of freedom in the growing-up process. And it is, to no small degree, the effect of the great and increasing economic power enjoyed by youth.

The young slowly are capturing an ever-growing share of the nation's market, both through their own purchasing power and, more important, through effective dictation to parents. Financial columnist Sylvia Porter, calling the teen-age market "a most enticing prospect" for retailers, estimates it at a "fabulous $10 billion a year, of which $3 billion goes for girls' clothing alone."

This teen-age tyranny is not, of course, the outcome of a conscious play for power; it is, rather, in an affluent society, a mutiny of the bountiful.

But the economic factor is only one symptom of a serious condition. False, or distorted, permissiveness has moved from the

[1] From article by Grace and Fred M. Hechinger. New York *Times Magazine*. p 27+. Mr. 19, '61. Reprinted by permission. Fred M. Hechinger is education editor of the New York *Times*.

home to the schools where, in some instances, pupils are asked whether or not they approve of such rules as the honor system. In extreme cases, they even are asked whether the curriculum meets with their favor.

Teen-age tyranny is reinforced by the pseudopsychological jargon that did so much harm to American education by equating adult guidance with authoritarian despotism. To prevent youngsters from aping anything that "is done" by "the peer group" is considered reactionary and repressive. Those parents who have not been indoctrinated by academic theorists are being "reached" by television's many psychological teen-operas in which youngsters play their tyrannical role to the hilt. . . .

In such an atmosphere, it is hardly surprising that teen-agers have come to dominate American cultural tastes, at least in much of the mass market. The teen-age tribal beat of popular music haunts the radio. . . .

Of course, much of the teen-age influence on the radio and record industry is to be attributed to the efforts of good salesmen, who know a potential market when they see one. Since they correctly estimate that the most doubtful tastes of the least sophisticated of the group will prevail, they appeal to that element.

But, whatever the explanation, there is little excuse for some of the wailing distortions that contaminate the air. Nor is it easy to find an alibi for those television "productions" that show hordes of awkward, self-conscious youngsters milling around a dance floor and making a spectacle of adolescent romance.

Even the most respectable adult, mass-circulation magazines have blossomed forth with lengthy columns about teen "problems," running the gamut from dating to going steady. They are generally written by, or ghosted for, those depressingly look-alike idols of teen-agers, the disk jockeys and "actors." The language, though unimaginatively wholesome, is always on the verge of the ungrammatical and in that teen-jargon which has been creeping into much "adult" advertising copy, as well.

Teen influence on the culture may be a slow subversion; the economic domination is quite overt. The makers of leotards, ballet slippers and Bermuda shorts know and cherish the story. The boom in snack foods and hero sandwiches is merely another chapter of the same tale. Few parents of today's teen-agers suspected, when their babies were in diapers, how expensive the teen years would be and how persuasive salesmen of the teen products would become.

There is nothing basically wrong with the desire to provide teen-agers with attractive things—until it gets out of hand. The teen charge accounts are an example. They assume that few parents are reactionary (or courageous) enough to prevent their children's extravagance. . . .

Parents often find it hard to say No to their children—not because they don't realize that it may be unwise to make certain concessions, but rather because they fear loss of social status among parents of other teen-agers.

This is especially true among parents who had few outward "advantages" in their own youth; they may want to buy precarious prestige and status by permitting their children to have the status symbols of the gang.

Naturally, adolescents are quick to exploit this parental attitude. How contagious this national weakness tends to be was shown when the small son of a foreign diplomat, stationed in New York, made the rounds of his American neighbors and told them that his father was "un-American" because he refused to buy a television set.

Status-seeking is not the whole story, however. Also to blame are the uncritical philosophy of permissiveness, introduced in the twenties, and a misinterpretation of the meaning of democracy, both in the home and in the school. Today, adults who ought to establish standards of adolescent behavior frequently resort to that convenient substitute for policy-making: the opinion poll.

A group of educators recently asked tots in the second grade whether they thought they were learning what they needed most to know. School "administrators" have tried to determine, by way of majority opinion, whether today's high school students should be allowed to smoke in school and, if so, what kind of special smoking rooms ought to be provided. . . .

In many communities, high school almost invariably means car ownership. Last fall, the opening of a new public high school in Norwalk, Connecticut, led to so vast a traffic jam that many commuters missed their trains.

When Norwalk's police chief asked that the school authorities limit student use of cars, a Board of Education spokesman said he could do nothing about it since anybody over sixteen is legally entitled to drive. Norwalk's adults "compromised" by taking earlier trains.

The news from Norwalk brought testimony of similar dilemmas from other parts of the country, including complaints about the "need" for expensive parking lots for new schools. When one community urged that this noneducational expense be covered by charging parking fees, the school superintendent said plaintively that this might lead to student parking in residential neighborhoods. Nobody considered it possible to lay down rules and enforce them.

This spectacle of adult helplessness goes on in the face of a recent study showing a direct relationship between students' use of cars and failure in their school work. Moreover, the National Safety Council reports that in 1959 teen-agers were involved in about twice as many accidents as their numbers would warrant. . . .

In its total effect, teen-age tyranny is not merely an inconvenience; it can be desperately harmful to the adolescents themselves. In extreme cases, it leads to heartbreak and ruined lives. Members of a parents' committee in an upper-middle-class commuter town recently complained "in confidence" that their small high school had seen more than ten "forced marriages" in one term. But those who wanted to counteract the dangerous trend by taking open measures of education and discipline were met with violent protest.

The hectic search for "popularity," says school psychologist John J. Morgenstern in the *Journal of the National Education Association,* leads to such as this: approved dating for nine-year-olds, so that they will be "ready for junior high school" and won't feel "left out." An elementary school principal comments, "I don't like it, but my PTA wants me to have fifth and sixth grade dances, and sometimes the fourth grade is invited to even out the number of boys and girls." But too many school authorities who "don't like it" lack the guts to be right rather than unpopular. . . .

Instead of protecting the teen-ager from the pressure of his peers, adults permit the pressure to become the accepted norm. . . .

A further danger signal is the increase of delinquency—not in the slums, where economic conditions make it explicable, but in the well-to-do suburbs. Last year, summer residents in one fashionable New York commuter town were shocked to find that teen-agers had been stealing cars from the railroad parking lot; it was their favorite relief from boredom.

In Englewood, New Jersey, seventeen youths were arrested after a long period of housebreaking, in which they had totaled $10,000 worth of loot. Most of the young burglars admitted having liberal allowances from home but went on their lawless sprees "just for kicks and because it was thrilling."

Westchester County's District Attorney last year issued a report on 251 persons, most of them in their teens and some as young as thirteen, who had used an extensive assortment of narcotics regularly at dances, club meetings, and parties. Some of these gatherings had been held in homes while parents were absent.

The youngsters came from well-to-do communities, from Port Chester to Pelham, and were joined regularly by "guests" from Fairfield County and New York City. According to a New York *Times* report, most of them were "high school and college students from prosperous families."

When one of the boys confessed, his father shouted: "I should take you by the throat and kill you. I have given you everything. Where have I failed?"

One experienced educator replies that this father and other parents like him have failed exactly because they have given their children everything. . . .

It is not easy for parents, in a prosperous society, to limit their generosity toward their children. Much of their desire to give is rooted in genuine love. But, at least in part, the excess of giving springs from feelings of guilt: It is a material substitute for lack of personal attention.

What can be done to halt a pernicious trend? Psychologist Morgenstern says:

Our child-rearing methods emphasize development of the individual so much that many parents find it difficult to apply sensible limits to children under twelve, and even more difficult as the youngsters reach adolescence and make their strongest bids for independence and feel the strongest need for conformity to their peer groups.

Increasingly, the experts are therefore abandoning the old extremes of permissiveness. They warn that, in the absence of adult "laws," the only law tends to become that of the lowest common adolescent denominator. The challenge of the "peers" is to explore the limits to which one dares go. The "dare" then becomes the tribal substitute for law, and the only punishment is to be considered "chicken" or to be hurt. Undoubtedly, the majority of teen-agers would prefer to have an "out" rather than to be dragged along by the dictatorial tribe.

Ironically, many articulate teen-agers try to tell their elders that they really don't enjoy their own regime. When recent years brought about a tightening of academic requirements in the schools, many students responded with enthusiasm and gratitude to hard work, intellectual challenge and the sensible new government by adult law. At a teen-age convocation of the Wayne County (Michigan) Camp Association last fall, the youngsters agreed that "teen-agers are punished by being pampered," and that they are "led to become accustomed to too much too soon."

One danger is that some panicky adults will try to cope with the teen-age tyranny by attacking the symptoms rather than the source of the disease. Others, attuned to the current faith in the magic of public relations, think that the "problems" can be made to appear insignificant by simply playing up "good news" about teen-agers.

The latter course is clearly no solution at all. As for the former, experts are convinced that no remedy can be found in a primitive "get tough" policy, such as is advocated in legislative proposals to introduce corporal punishment in the schools.

What the experts do want is a reestablishment of sensible adult authority, coupled with admirable adult values.

"An adolescent has the right to know the best judgment of those whom he respects as to what his strengths and weaknesses are," says Eric W. Johnson, head of the Germantown (Pennsylvania) Friends Junior High School.

Turning to the specific problem of establishing rules, Mr. Johnson adds: "Teen-agers appreciate a clear understanding about the time of return (from a party) and a definite word (from the parents) so that they do not have to make the self-belittling decision that it's now time to go home."

In exercising their authority, parents must, of course, make it clear that they are doing so not just because they are bigger and stronger, but because they have the benefit of greater experience and the burden of greater responsibility.

By taking this view, they inevitably will encounter "crises" and opposition. They will find it especially difficult to remain firm when the majority of parents in the neighborhood continues to be excessively permissive. On this problem—not of keeping up with the Joneses, but of keeping the Joneses in line—specific advice comes from Dr. Benjamin Spock [noted authority on child care]:

> The parents' best defense is to keep in touch with the parents of their children's friends, and to devote PTA meetings to discussion of such matters. . . . It's often a surprise and a pleasure to find that most of them share your point of view (contrary to reports from your children), and that everyone is ready to come to a neighborhood agreement. Such a code is a comfort to the children, too, because it assures them that they will not be ridiculously out of line.

Naturally, the courage to establish laws and regulations is needed as much in the school as in the home. If cars are harmful to high school learning and mores, for instance, there is practical precedent for law enforcement: Some of the best colleges, including Princeton, have had the courage to outlaw cars, simply by basing their decision on the fact that it is better for education.

There is steadily growing agreement among today's experts that the extreme permissiveness of a generation ago has done great harm to teen-agers. In his new book, *The Education of Nations,* Robert Ulich, James Bryant Conant Professor Emeritus at Harvard University, asks:

> Would it not be more conducive to a person's development if he were more free when he could profit from his freedom, namely, as a young man, or woman, and more controlled when control might be at the right place, namely, as an adolescent?

Professor Ulich urges today's parents and teachers to understand that the difficult business of growing up demands "not only freedom from false authority, but also respect for rightful authority."

If adult authority is one part of the fight against teen-age tyranny, the establishment of challenging goals is equally important. Dr. Edward D. Eddy, Jr., president of Chatham College, recently conducted a study of college students on many campuses. He observed that teen-agers, perhaps misinterpreting the psychologists' stress on individualism and "child-centered" schools, have developed a dangerous streak of "privatism." Their key question is: "What's in it for me?"

But the antidote, as Dr. Eddy points out and as recent events have underlined, is in kindling in young people a joyful sense of their talents and the expectation of excitement as the reward for effort and service. That this is not a Utopian idea has been demonstrated by the electric response of young people across the country to such challenges as the Peace Corps, and by the less spectacular but equally important involvement of teen-agers in science projects.

It is no accident that so much of the "good news" about teen-agers has come from the science laboratories, where laws and regulations are adult-established and clearly defined, and where adult knowledge is expected and respected. It is a ready hint as to how parents and teachers, willing to risk the loss of "palship" by acting like responsible adults, can make adolescence a step toward growing up, not a privilege to be exploited.

WHERE IS THE COLLEGE GENERATION HEADED? [2]

The conflict of the generations is neither a new nor a particularly American story, but it is perhaps exacerbated by the self-consciousness and the partial segregation of teen-age culture, to such an extent that both old and young are exceptionally vulnerable to their mutual criticisms. I do not care to add to the complacency of my agemates who, from their clubs, pulpits, and other rostrums, attack the alleged "softness" of the young, whom they have themselves brought up, while failing to see the

[2] From article by David Riesman, noted sociologist, formerly at the University of Chicago and now professor of social sciences at Harvard University, and senior author of *The Lonely Crowd*. *Atlantic Monthly*. 207:39-45. Ap. '61. Reprinted by permission. These observations were first published in January 1958 in the *Chicago Review* and brought up to date for publication in the *Atlantic Monthly*.

difficulties young people face today precisely because the manifest hardships with which earlier Americans coped have been, for millions, attenuated. These hardships cannot be artificially restored, at least for people over twelve; however, I believe that college students are now beginning to find new ways to become active politically, and hence responsible humanly.

It is easy to underestimate the importance of this in America, where students until recently did not play the role in politics that they do in Latin America, Turkey, Korea, or Japan. For, the cadres of the disinherited who once helped power political change in this country are diminished in numbers and even more diminished in leadership, now that nearly every bright, motivated boy gets funneled into college if he wants to go. Thus, our expanding colleges absorb increasingly large fractions of the available idealism and dynamism of our society. And at the same time . . . many students are not attracted by the traditional goals of commercial or professional ambition; the best of them have no love for the status quo. Rejecting careerism, they often choose familism instead. But shaken out of this, either by the open discrimination felt by Negroes or the subtler dissatisfaction with contemporary life felt by whites, they comprise a privileged minority, ignorant of its strength, yet capable of change.

College students today often act as if they believed that work in large organizations, and beyond that, work in general, could not be basically satisfying (or, at times, even honest), but is primarily a way to earn a living, to find a place in the social order, and to meet nice or not-so-nice people. This is a conclusion which is partly projected upon the occupational scene as the result of their experience with the curriculum in college and university, and also as the result of experience with college and university as organizations which are viewed as bureaucratic, monolithic, and unchangeable by many students.

I do not think it is the primary task of education to prepare students for their later occupational roles, or, indeed, any narrowly specialized roles, nor to teach them to enjoy work regardless of its quality and meaning. Rather, the relation of education to later life should be a dialectical and critical one. If, however, one result of going to college is to become alienated from work per se and defeatist about the possibility of altering one's relation to it, then it seems to me one ought to reexamine academic institutions themselves and see whether anything in them, or in one's own attitudes, or in both might be changed.

In the spring of 1955, several hundred interviews were done (at the behest of *Time* magazine) with seniors at twenty colleges throughout the country, most of them colleges of distinction. The seniors were supposed to be reasonably representative, but what this was taken to mean and how it was applied at different colleges and universities varied greatly. A good many student leaders were chosen, a good many bright people, but hardly any women were included (a questionnaire circulated by *Mademoiselle* gave me somewhat comparable data concerning college women). When I first examined the interviews, and now again when I have once more gone over them, I have been struck by what appears to be a not quite conscious ambivalence toward work in large organizations. Nevertheless, the majority are planning to enter large organizations in pursuit of their careers: big corporations, big governments, big law offices, and so on. Only a few seek independence in their work, either in terms of old-fashioned ideals of entrepreneurship or in terms of the desire to become a foreign correspondent, to enter politics, or to follow some other individualistic or exotic calling. (Moreover, hardly anyone expresses resentment against his prospective army service on the ground that the army is a large organization; there is no eagerness for service, but rather resignation to it as one of the givens of life.)

And yet, when these young people are asked about their lives outside of work, a very different picture emerges. There, bigness and scale are definitely not valued. Only a tiny fraction want to head for the metropolis, even if their careers might make such a location convenient. They want the suburbs—not later, after some bachelor independence in the big city, but now, on graduation. The great majority either are already married or plan to get married soon (even if there is no special one in mind at the moment); they plan to start having children at once and to begin building a community-centered life in the suburbs. They envisage a two-car, but usually not a two-career, family, in which the prospective wife will be active in the Parent-Teacher Association, with assistance from the husband, and in which both spouses will concern themselves with a manageable bit of real estate in a suburban neighborhood in which they can at once be active and hope to make a difference. It does not occur to them that they might be gifted and energetic enough to make a difference even in a big city. Rather, they want to be able to work through a face-to-face group—the postcollegiate fraternity of the small suburbs.

Correspondingly, the very emphasis on family life, which is one of the striking and, in so many ways, attractive qualities of young people today, is an implicit rejection of large organization. The suburban family, with its garden, its barbecue, its lack of privacy in the open-plan house, is itself a manifesto of decentralization, even though it makes use of centralized services such as television, clinics, chain stores, and *House Beautiful.* The wish to build a nest, even if a somewhat transient one, is a striking feature of the interviews, in contrast with the wish to build a fortune or a career, which might have dominated some comparable interviews a generation earlier.

This pattern—the acceptance of large organizations, combined with tacit and uncrystallized resistance to them—appears not only in the respondents' emphasis on the family but also in what they say about their plans and attitudes toward their future work. I get a sense from the material, and from other comparable data, of a certain withdrawal of emotional adherence from work. To be sure, it has become fashionable to speak of one's work or other activities in deprecatory terms and to adopt a pose of relative indifference to the larger goals of an organization. In an era of political, economic, and cultural salesmanship, such deprecation is a way of guarding against being exploited for ends outside one's self. It is as if one had constantly to conduct psychological warfare against an outside enemy. But, as in any such process, students become to some extent the victims of their own defenses. They come to believe that work cannot really be worth doing for its own sake, whether or not it is done on behalf of a large, impersonal organization. They fear overcommitment to their work even while they are at the workplace. In the course of getting rid of earlier collegiate or rah-rah enthusiasm, these young people have come to feel that work is not worth even their part-time devotion, and perhaps that nothing, except the family, deserves their wholehearted allegiance.

We see the same attitudes, of course, among the junior echelons now engaged in work. One hears them talk of their benevolent company as "a mink-lined rattrap," or speak of "the rat race," or refer to fights over principles as "ruckuses" or "blowups"—if somebody cares, he is said to "blow his top." In a number of business novels, of which *The Man in the Gray Flannel Suit* is representative, it is taken for granted that a sensible fellow, and, indeed, an honest one, will prefer suburban domesticity and a quiet niche to ulcerous competition for large business stakes, despite the view from the top and the interesting climb.

Attitudes such as these are of course an aspect of a general cultural shift, not confined to students and not confined to those who seek employment in large organizations; similar attitudes turn up in some measure even among those who, studiously avoiding such organizations, look for a professional career in which they hope to be their own masters. Scholars, for example, are not immune to distaste for their work, nor are architects or physicians. But, while I do not intend to imply that a life without any boredom is conceivable, except for a very stupid person, still, I think we are witnessing a silent revolution against work on the part of even those relatively privileged groups who have been free to choose their work and to exercise some freedom in the doing of it. This reflects, in part, the fact that much work is meaningless per se, save as a source of income, prestige, and sociability, but it also indicates, as I have already implied, that people too readily accept their work as it comes, without the hope of making it more meaningful.

Not all large organizations are alike . . . and, of course, not all positions in them are alike. Many, although their top executives clamor for creativity and independence of mind, largely manage to process these qualities out of "their" people in the lower ranks. Others stockpile talent and expect it to keep as gold keeps at Fort Knox. Still others make products or provide services which are either antisocial or useless. But here and there one finds companies which face real and not contrived problems and apply to them an intelligence which is often remarkably disinterested and, in the best sense of the term, "academic." Young people in search of challenge and development would do well to seek out such relatively productive climates, rather than to assume offhand that these (as is true of so many brand-name products) are all alike except for the advertising and the label. And this search is necessary precisely because many of the motives which impelled work in the older generation have fortunately become attenuated, motives such as money for its own sake, power, and fame—goals, that is, whose emptiness became evident with their attainment. Our industrial and commercial plant no longer "needs" such compulsive attachments to work, which are based not on any genuine creative impulse but on the drying up of other alternatives and on the pressure of extrinsic standards of value.

There is a further issue concerning work in large organizations where, again, differentiation is required. I refer to the conception that work in organizations requires surrender of independence of judgment, if not of integrity. When I was in college, there was a prevalent feeling among the more sensitive that this was true only of business and commercial organizations, not of governmental or philanthropic ones, and young men debated whether they would enter Wall Street and make money, or enter government or teaching and be saved. This dichotomy has in large measure vanished, although traces of it do survive among the less cynical. For instance, I have known many graduate students in social psychology who believe that if they teach, they can be honest, but that if they work in market research, they will serve manipulation and corruption and will have no power over their own work. Such judgments oversimplify the ethical dilemmas of any calling and are, in addition, snobbish; one can find hucksterism (often hypocritically veiled) among academic people in search of reputations, grants, and promotions, as well as among market researchers and other businessmen.

Indeed, I am inclined to think that, at present, many observant young people do not need to be persuaded of this; many are actually overpersuaded to the point of believing that every occupation is a racket and that at best some of the racketeers are less pious about it than others. And this, I suspect, is one of the reasons they tend to withdraw emotional allegiance from their work—with the impression that they have no control over it anyway, that all is in the hands of the mysterious men upstairs who run the show. If there is greater wisdom in their belief that all occupations, like all forms of power, are corrupting in some degree, there is also greater resignation, greater passivity and fatalism.

Where are such attitudes learned and confirmed? Even at some of the leading colleges, the more intellectual colleges, the colleges which produce literary magazines, the relation of students to the curriculum has a certain alienated quality, in the sense that the students do not believe they have any control over their own education.

In the last few years I have visited a number of colleges of high quality, colleges which turn out eminent professional men, scholars, and scientists, and I have made it my business to talk with students informally, to read their student newspapers and, where possible, student council reports. At a number of these institutions, the livelier students complain of the educational fare they are getting, of the very little contact the curriculum makes with the problems that are meaningful to them. Sometimes they feel that opportunities for a civilized and intellectual life on campus are wanting—for example, that there are few inviting places to study or to talk, that social pressures in dormitories force any intellectual life out of the group setting, that student publications are either dominated by the school administration or devoted to campus news and trivia, that the bookstore is inadequate, or that the library is geared to meet research needs rather than to attract undergraduate browsers. They often feel that they have no access to the faculty for other than merely routine matters. Sometimes students complain about the prerequisites of a department, which serve its monopolistic aims or protect its mediocre teachers from boycott rather than serve any defensible pedagogic aims.

Yet, when I ask such students what they have done about these things, they are surprised at the very thought that they could do anything. They think I am joking when I suggest that, if things came to the worst, they could picket! They think I am wholly unrealistic when I say that many on the faculty might welcome student initiative in revising the curriculum, or that it might be possible to raise modest sums of money among alumni or others to bring visiting lecturers or poets to the campus, or to furnish commodious rooms for interest-group meetings. When I tell them that the Harvard house plan came about in considerable measure because of the report of a student council committee in 1926 which caught the attention of the philanthropist Edward Harkness, they shrug. That must have been a golden era, they say; nothing like that could happen now. Of course, as long as they think that, they will conduct themselves accordingly.

Why is it that students, often so precocious about many things—about each other, about sex, about their families, and occasionally even about national and world affairs—are comparatively inattentive to what concerns them as closely as does their curriculum?

For one thing, it seems to me that students do not want to believe that their activities might make a difference, because, in a way, they profit from their lack of commitment to what they are doing. I do not mean that they are not industrious students; they go through the required motions of working, but they seldom get really involved with the content of their courses. It is here that the better, more conscientious students sabotage their own education and restrict production; true enough, they turn out the credits and the grades, but they do not believe that it really matters in any fundamental sense what they think and feel.

When I have discussed this with students, they have often told me that it doesn't pay to be too interested in anything, because then one is tempted to spend too much time on it, at the expense of that optimal distribution of effort which will produce the best grades—and after all, they do have to get into medical school, keep their scholarship, and "please the old man." Now, I am convinced that grades contaminate education—they are a kind of currency which, like money, gets in the way of students' discovering their intellectual interests—but here, too, the students in their realism are being somewhat unrealistic. They assume, for one thing, that it is hopeless to try to alter the curriculum so that it might penalize them less for serious interest in one topic at the expense of others, or so that there might be more emphasis on reading and discussion and more opportunity for independent thinking. And here, also, the students have a distorted image of what will actually make an impression on their teachers either now or later. On this point, I have some evidence to back me up.

After I had tried in vain for some time to persuade graduate students at Chicago that they could be more independent in their course and thesis work without any heroism, any martyrdom, there was a thesis done by a student which documented my arguments. The student went around to the departments and asked them which students in recent years they had recommended for jobs or advanced training or fellowships and which they had not. Then he interviewed some of these students in various categories of faculty blessing or disapproval, looked at their grades, and so on. He concluded that those students frequently fared best who were not too obedient, who did not get an undiluted, uncomplicated, straight-A record. (The straight-A students, in fact, sometimes slipped away without anyone's noticing.)

The students who were most successful were a bit rebellious, a bit offbeat, though not entirely "goof-offs"; these were the students likely to appeal to a faculty member who had not entirely repressed a rebelliousness of his own that had led him to be a teacher in the first place, a faculty member who was looking for signs of life, even if they gave him a bit of trouble at times. To be sure, such a student had to do well in something to earn this response, but he was often better off to have written a brilliant paper or two than to have divided his time, as an investment banker his money, among a variety of subjects. Those students who were the most self-consciously opportunistic and realistic in allocating their time and emotion were in fact sacrificing themselves unprofitably, suffering not only now, during the studies which they regarded as an anteroom to life, but later on as well.

Now, not all departments at Chicago were alike in this matter; some gave more play to defiance and deviation than others. Moreover, this study encompassed only the social science departments. No doubt departments and institutions differ very much in this respect. But that is just the point I want to emphasize: by concluding prematurely that all organizations are alike, that all demand the same kind of conformity, students not only surrender the chance to experience an atmosphere that is freer and more conducive to their own development but perpetuate a myth that then controls their passage through jobs in later life. If the University of Chicago or even one's department itself cannot be changed from below, how can one expect to change General Motors, or *Look* magazine, or the big hospitals of San Francisco? And if that is so, then why not settle for the fringe benefits, for a position of moderate respectability and adequate, if not dazzling salary?

At work here is a characteristic social pattern in which individuals, hesitant to reveal feelings they have scarcely voiced to themselves, are misled about what in effect could be done if they expressed themselves, thereby discovering others who might share their views. (Sociologists refer to this process as "pluralistic ignorance.") Leadership, of course, whether in politics or in other affairs, often serves to help a group change its apparent mood to conform to its actual or potential but repressed views, but leadership also may, and frequently does, serve to continue enforcing the repression. Even in a large organization, radical and what were previously regarded as "impossible" changes come about almost instantaneously once people discover that views they had previously regarded as unacceptable or idiosyncratic are in fact widely shared.

The students know that there are many decisions out of their conceivable control, decisions upon which their lives and fortunes truly depend. But what I am contending is that this truth, this insight, is overgeneralized, and that, being believed, it becomes more and more "true." Not only do we fail to spot those instances in which intervention might change things quite substantially, but we fail to develop the competence and the confidence in ourselves that are necessary to any large endeavor. In that sense, despite our precociousness, we fail to grow up; we remain the children of organization, not the masters of it.

For Americans, there is something paradoxical about this development. Americans in the past have not been overimpressed by mechanical achievements. Workers in a steel mill are not awed by the giant rollers, and we take for granted that we are not awed by any large physical construction made by our hands and brains. Contrary to the prevalent impression abroad that we are slaves to our machines, we are actually relatively uninvolved with them, and we surely do not feel dominated by them. But it seems to be different with the organizational machines. These are as much the product of our thinking and our imagination as any technological feat; yet, as Erich Fromm [the eminent psychologist] has said, we worship like idolaters the product we have created, an image not of stone but of other images.

It is a commonplace observation that in organizational life we use arguments to convince others which we think will appeal to them, even though they do not convince us. We try to persuade people to behave justly to Negroes because "discrimination makes the United States look bad in the Cold War," as if that were why we ourselves behaved decently. Or we persuade businessmen to give money to colleges for all sorts of public relations reasons, playing on their fear of radicalism or Federal control or whatnot, whereas we ourselves devote our lives to education for quite different reasons. All arguments of this nature have two qualities: they patronize the other person and they perpetuate "pluralistic ignorance." It can be contended that there may be occasions when we must appeal to others as they are, not as we should like them to be; when there is not time for idealism. But, in our realism, we often make mistakes about what others will actually respond to, and we sacrifice the integrity and clarity of our argument to our false image of what will go over. The result: we conclude that one cannot be honest while working for an organization, that one can be honest only when one is at home with one's family in the suburbs.

There is another result as well; namely, that we often end up in doubt as to what we ourselves think. We come to believe what we say to others and thus become "more sincere" in the subjective sense, but at the price of becoming still more confused as to what is actually so: we are the first victims of our own propaganda. No wonder we end up without emotional ties to what we do, for it is no longer we who do it, but some limited part of ourselves, playing a role. Not recognizing that we in some measure have done this to ourselves, we attribute to organizations the power and the primacy we have lost. And then, as I have said, we strike back, not directly, but by a kind of emotional attrition in which we lend to our work willingness without enthusiasm, conscientiousness without creativity.

I am sure that many college students who are not only serious but dedicated know this as well as I do. Such students have managed to make college serve their purposes and have in this way gained some rational confidence that they will be able to do the same in the organizations they will enter later, whether these are universities, business concerns, or the many voluntary organizations through which we Americans carry out much of our communal work. What I have principally sought to do in these remarks is to encourage greater and more differentiated realism than many young people already possess, a realism which does not take for granted the social structures which seem so impressive but which looks for the points of leverage where one's own effort, joined to that of others similarly freed from mythology, might make a difference. In many situations, there is more leeway than students think, and college is a good place to find this out.

THE STRATEGY OF A SIT-IN [3]

If no wool-hat politicians from the rural counties are loitering about with their ears cocked for subversive conversation, both Negro and white natives are apt to boast that Atlanta is "the New York of the South."

One morning last March, sophisticated Atlanta was rudely jarred by the realization that it was like New York in ways it had never particularly noticed before: its Negro minority was not at all timid about expressing its dissatisfaction and demanding action in no uncertain terms. In fact, there in the morning Atlanta *Constitution* was a full-page advertisement entitled "An Appeal for Human Rights," and the list of rights the Negroes said they wanted ranged all the way from the right of attending the public schools of Georgia on a nonsegregated basis to being admitted to hospitals, concerts, and restaurants on the same basis as anybody else. The home-bound commuters got the same message in a full-page advertisement in the evening *Journal*, which, according to its masthead, "Covers Dixie Like the Dew."

[3] From article by C. Eric Lincoln, professor of social philosophy, Clark College, Atlanta, Georgia. *Reporter*. 24:20-3. Ja. 5, '61. Copyright 1961 by The Reporter Magazine Company. Reprinted by permission.

The advertisement, signed by six Negro students representing the six Negro colleges in Atlanta, said in part:

> We, the students of the six affiliated institutions forming the Atlanta University Center—Clark, Morehouse, Morris Brown and Spelman colleges, Atlanta University and the Interdenominational Theological Center—have joined our hearts, minds and bodies in the cause of gaining those rights which are inherently ours as members of the human race and as citizens of the United States. . . .
>
> We do not intend to wait placidly for those rights which are already legally and morally ours. . . . Today's youth will not sit by submissively, while being denied all rights, privileges, and joys of life. . . .
>
> We must say in all candor that we plan to use every legal and nonviolent means at our disposal to secure full citizenship rights as members of this great Democracy. . . .

The reaction in Atlanta, a city known for its more or less amicable race relations, was swift and vigorous. In the white community there was genuine amazement over the dissatisfaction of the Negro students. After all, in Atlanta many Negroes own expensive homes, run substantial businesses, and practice the professions with a high degree of respect in the community at large.

Predictably, white reaction polarized along urban-rural political lines. Mayor William B. Hartsfield, whose qualifications as a hardheaded southern liberal are rated high by many of the most militant advocates of Negro rights, praised the statement and said that it "performs the constructive service of letting the white community know what others are thinking."

But a few blocks away in the state capitol, Governor Ernest Vandiver denounced the student appeal as a "left-wing statement . . . calculated to breed dissatisfaction, discontent, discord and evil." The Georgia governor had been elected on a platform of total segregation by a predominantly rural electorate voting under Georgia's so-called county-unit system. . . . The governor did go so far as to admit that the appeal for human rights was "skillfully prepared"—so well prepared in fact, that "Obviously, it was not written by students.". . .

The governor could have been more generous in his estimate of the quality of education in Georgia. As far as Negroes are concerned, Atlanta, with six private and church-related institutions of higher learning, has long been a unique educational center. It is estimated that at least 10 per cent of all Negro Ph.D.'s in America received their undergraduate training in Atlanta. And the students of the Atlanta University Center were soon to exhibit a remarkable degree of skill at dramatizing their determination to have the rights to which they feel entitled.

First Skirmishes

The sit-in movement in Atlanta was born in a corner drugstore opposite the Atlanta University Center, when a handful of students from the several Negro colleges found themselves discussing the sit-ins already in progress in North Carolina and elsewhere. A mass meeting at Atlanta University early last March [1960] resulted in the formation of a Committee on Appeal for Human Rights, which several days later drew up the statement enumerating their grievances and calling upon "all people in authority . . . all leaders in civic life . . . and all people of goodwill to assert themselves and abolish these injustices."

To test the receptiveness of white Atlantans to the attempted desegregation of public and semipublic facilities, the students sought to attend a musical at the city auditorium with tickets for orchestra seats ordered in advance; and they "sat in" for service at a lunch counter at Rich's, the largest department store in the Southeast. At the municipal auditorium they were permitted to occupy the seats for which they held tickets, but the section in which they sat was promptly designated a Negro section by the management, and seating continued on a de facto segregated basis. At Rich's the students were served on March 3 and 4, but thereafter, and without prior notice, they were refused. The Appeal for Human Rights followed, but neither the newspaper advertisements nor attempts at negotiation with Rich's and the other major downtown stores produced results. . . .

It is generally assumed that from 70 to 90 per cent of the Negroes in Atlanta's business and professional class have maintained accounts . . . [at Rich's]. When no satisfactory agreement could be reached with the management of the store, the students threw picket lines in front of it and urged all Negroes to cancel their accounts and practice "selective purchasing"—

that is, to spend their money somewhere else. This was to be the first in a series of skirmishes with the giant store, a kind of field maneuver in preparation for an all-out campaign in the fall.

By the time the colleges were closed for summer vacation, the student movement had taken on some of the aspects of a permanent organization. The Committee on Appeal for Human Rights had developed into a kind of general staff, and several operating committees with specific functions had been set up under its aegis. A Student-Adult Liaison Committee had been established to interpret the student movement to the Negro community and to enlist its support. On this committee were business executives, college presidents, professors, lawyers, other Negro leaders, and students.

The adult members of the liaison committee also served in an advisory capacity on request, but they were excluded from all student meetings dealing with policy and strategy. As one student leader has explained, "We preferred not to embarrass or otherwise discompose our adult leaders; they may have vested interests or personal obligations which may make it difficult for them to share directly in our deliberations, or in our strategy and the implementation of policy." Nevertheless, the sit-ins got overwhelming support from Negro adults, both direct and indirect. For one thing, during the summer a great many adults learned to get along without the convenience of charge accounts at the downtown stores. One group of businessmen underwrote a modest newspaper called the Atlanta *Inquirer,* edited by a college professor and largely staffed by students.

After most of the college students had scattered for their summer vacations, a switch in tactics directed the summer "field maneuvers" at chain grocery stores that have outlets in Negro neighborhoods but discriminate against Negroes in their employment practices. Except for "selective purchasing," the main campaign against the downtown stores was postponed until fall.

The summer "maneuvers" were directed mainly at units of Colonial Stores and at some smaller businesses located in areas with from 95 to 100 per cent Negro patronage. When the stores refused to negotiate with the students on the question of hiring Negroes above the level of menials, picket lines were organized and a selective purchasing campaign was urged upon Negro housewives. The chief target, a Colonial store near the heart of the Negro business district on the city's northwest side, suddenly "closed for remodeling." A few days later it reopened with Negroes upgraded in three departments. Shortly thereafter a second store in the Colonial chain hired a Negro cashier and a Negro butcher. Two smaller stores had either already employed Negro salespersons or did so immediately after Colonial changed its policies.

Logistics and Deployment

What came to be referred to as the "Fall Campaign" got under way immediately after the reopening of the colleges in mid-September. This time the main sit-in targets were in the heart of the Atlanta shopping district. Because of its size and its alleged "leadership" in the maintenance of segregated facilities, Rich's became once again the prime objective. Encouraged, however, by the fact that in the seven months since the sit-ins had begun in Greensboro, North Carolina, 112 southern cities had desegregated lunch counters, the students added Davison-Paxon, the second largest store in Atlanta, as well as drug chains such as Lane-Rexall and Walgreen and the dime and variety stores, including Woolworth, Kress, W. T. Grant, McCrory, Newberry, and H. L. Green. Accommodations were requested at *all* facilities—lunch counters, rest rooms, and in the case of the department stores, restaurants and dining rooms.

The stores refused to negotiate with the students, and beginning on October 19 a succession of sit-ins harassed the downtown merchants and brought out scores of extra police and plainclothes detectives. By Friday, October 21, hundreds of students had launched attacks in coordinated waves. Service to *anyone* at eating facilities in the stores involved had all but ended, and sixty-one students, one white heckler, and Dr. Martin Luther King were all in jail. Under a truce called by Mayor Hartsfield everyone was out of jail by Sunday morning except Dr. King. Negotiations between the merchants and the Student-Adult Liaison Committee were promised on the initiative of the mayor. When the truce ended thirty days later, no progress had been made in settling the impasse, and on November 25, the all-out attack was resumed. By mid-December, Christmas buying was down 16 per cent—almost $10 million below normal.

Both the Atlanta police and the merchants have been baffled by the students' apparent ability to appear out of nowhere armed with picket signs, and by the high degree of coordination with which simultaneous attacks were mounted against several stores at once. Even members of the Ku Klux Klan, dressed in full regalia and prepared to counterdemonstrate against the students, frequently found themselves wandering around the downtown streets bemused—always a jump or two behind the sit-in students. The secret of their easy mobility lay in the organization the students had perfected in anticipation of an extended siege.

Much of the credit for the development of the organizational scheme belongs to Lonnie King, a Morehouse student who is the recognized leader of the student movement in Atlanta, and his immediate "general staff." Policy-making is done by a board of about fifteen students, constituting the Committee on Appeal for Human Rights, which interprets and tries to make effective the wishes of the students of the six colleges who are loosely joined together in what is known as the Atlanta Student Movement. The committee is co-chaired by Lonnie King and Herschelle Sullivan, a twenty-two-year-old senior at Spelman College. Its executive officer has the rather whimsical title of "*le Commandante.*"

Le Commandante is Fred C. Bennette, a pre-theology student at Morris Brown College. The headquarters of the movement are in the basement of a church near the University Center, and Bennette arrives there promptly at seven o'clock each morning and goes through a stack of neatly typed reports covering the previous day's operations. On the basis of these reports, the strategy for the day is planned.

By eight o'clock the first contingent of volunteers for the day's assignment has arrived; there may be anywhere between twenty-five and a hundred students present. There is a brief devotional period, which usually concludes with a prayer that the white people of Georgia and throughout the United States will learn to overcome their prejudices, and that the students will be restrained, nonviolent, and loving in their attempts to establish human dignity in Georgia. After the devotions, the student volunteers may go to the church kitchen for coffee and doughnuts provided by various adult organizations. They are then likely to scatter about the church looking for places to study until they are summoned for duty.

Meanwhile, *le Commandante* and his staff are in conference. Robert ("Tex") Felder, deputy chief of operations and a . . . student at the Interdenominational Theological Center, will have arrived, as will a fellow student, the Reverend Otis Moss, who serves as field commander for the committee. Morris J. Dillard of Morehouse and James Felder of Clark College, who serve as co-chairmen of a subcommittee on public relations, will be on hand, and *le Commandante* will also expect to hear a report from a Clark College senior, Benjamin Brown, who keeps the organization's books and acts as its treasurer. Telephoned reports from senior intelligence officer Daniel Mitchell, a Clark junior (already at his post downtown), will describe the nature of the flow of traffic at each potential target.

"All Right, Let's Go"

The general staff having concluded its deliberations, a number of pickets selected on the basis of their class schedules and the nature of the day's objectives will be assembled and briefed by deputy commander Robert Felder. A large map dividing the downtown district into five areas is invariably consulted and an area commander is appointed for each operational district. Assignments fall into three categories: pickets (called by the students "picketeers"), sit-ins, and a sort of flying squad called "sit-and-runs." The objective of the sit-and-runs is simply to close lunch counters by putting in an appearance and requesting service. When the merchants discontinue service to all rather than serve the Negroes, the sit-and-runs move on to another target. The group designated "sit-ins" are prepared to contest their right to be served and are willing to go to jail if need be. Those volunteering for sit-in duty agree not to request bail if they are arrested.

By now it is nine or nine-thirty, and transportation has arrived. Cars provided without charge by funeral homes or other businesses as well as by individual housewives and some students are waiting to be loaded. The deputy commander provides each driver with a driver's orientation sheet outlining in detail the route to be followed by each driver, and the places where each of the respective groups of students are to be let out. The area commanders are given final instructions concerning the synchronization of the attack, and the cars move off, following different routes into the city.

In one of the last cars to leave headquarters will be the deputy field commander, who with a selected squad of "standbys" will be driven to his "field headquarters" on the "Ramparts," a designation referring to the steps of the Post Office annex across the street from Rich's department store.

Meanwhile, field commander Otis Moss is checking a communications code with Ernest Brown, an eighteen-year-old Morehouse junior, or one of the five other licensed radio operators who man a short-wave radio set up in the church nursery. When this has been attended to, commander Moss climbs into an ancient automobile equipped with a short-wave sending and receiving unit and heads for the downtown shopping district. He is accompanied by Robert Allen, eighteen, a Morehouse junior majoring in physics, whose job it will be to man the mobile radio unit.

The students have scarcely been deployed before a delivery truck arrives with a crate of apples and a dozen loaves of bread. These are from a small storekeeper who wants to contribute to the cause. Other gifts of food, cigarettes, and soft drinks arrive during the course of the morning. A housewife brings in a half dozen pies; an insurance executive calls to say that he will underwrite the cost of $115 worth of printing the students have contracted for. A small service station will give a hundred gallons of gasoline. All such gifts are recorded and notes of thanks are written to the donors by members of a subcommittee on community support. By eleven o'clock a group of churchwomen have arrived to prepare lunch for the students.

Reports from the field and area commanders begin to trickle in by radio and telephone. As the lunch hour nears, the volume of reports will increase to one every two or three minutes. The reports are typed and dated and placed on the desk of *le Commandante* by a corps of young women who serve as "communication aides." Duplicates are posted on the bulletin board and the students remaining at headquarters crowd around to watch the fortunes of their colleagues downtown. Here are two actual reports taken from the files and approved for publication by the security officer:

> 11/26/60 11:05 AM
>
> *From:* Captain Lenora Tait
>
> *To: le Commandante*
>
> Lunch counters at Rich's closed. Proceeded to alternative objective. Counters at Woolworth's also closed. Back to Rich's for picket duty. Ku Klux Klan circling Rich's in night gowns and dunce caps. "Looking good!"
>
> *From:* Gwendolyn Lee
>
> *To: le Commandante*
>
> Sign has been torn from the back of one of our white picketeers. He got another sign and returned to the line. Morale of white picketeers very good. Known heckler, an old man in a gray suit, is on the scene. White opposition increasing. Plainclothes detective made coordinator keep moving. All picketeers now in front of Rich's.

The white pickets referred to were from Emory University, a segregated Methodist college in Atlanta. White students from the University of Georgia have also joined the Negro students in the picket lines. . . . Support from adult Negroes is firm and consistent, and professional men and women have joined the students in the picket lines on "Doctors' Day," "Nurses' Day," and even "Professors' Day."

In some cases the students have been encouraged by white clerks and other personnel working in the very stores against which the sit-ins are directed. . . .

There seems little doubt that the efforts will be continued. The Negro students and their white and black allies are determined to keep on sitting in, sitting and running, and picketing until their battle is won.

[A major objective of the student sit-ins was achieved in September 1961, when many Atlanta stores desegregated eating places, rest rooms, and other facilities as a result of an agreement made in March 1961 between merchants and the Committee on Appeal for Human Rights. Rich's opened its restaurant, the

Magnolia Room, to Negroes. Desegregated also in 1961 were the University of Georgia, Georgia Institute of Technology, and four Atlanta high schools.—Ed.]

CAMPUS LIBERALS AND CONSERVATIVES [4]

I am on the inside of the student generation looking out, and I am sure of at least one thing: Perhaps because of age barriers, or superficial journalism, or because youth has failed to summarize its aspirations coherently, the elders who watch and anxiously analyze the development of my generation do not see us as we are.

In the past year, almost twenty articles have appeared in national liberal journals calling the new generation enthusiastic, bright, and liberal. Almost as many articles have sprung up in the conservative press calling us thrillingly conservative. If this is not evidence enough to demonstrate that men too often confuse what they see with what they wish to see, it is only necessary to note the doings of the House Un-American Activities Committee which believes that Communists are responsible for much of the current youthful unrest and turmoil. . . .

It is no accident that the HUAC-sponsored film, "Operation Abolition," has been of continuing interest to the American public. The film, which depicts youth as the pawn of an international Communist conspiracy, is significant not only because it has fired off heated debates in both the student and adult communities, and because it has distorted the threat of communism and sent many adults off on frightened, reckless campaigns against the Red menace, but also because the film and the response to it illustrate the severe psychological effect that the long, long cold war has had on the American consciousness. Americans are not used to living in a world so full of enemies. Some, in their fear, are beginning to equate any radical action with communism. No wonder that the rise of a militant younger generation is so disturbing to its elders.

Let us be clear, first of all, on this: The majority of American students are not active or even deeply interested in politics. Their

[4] From "Who Are the Student Boat-Rockers?" article by Thomas Hayden, former editor of the University of Michigan *Daily*, who has been active in liberal student movements and is now following developments in the South for Students for a Democratic Society. *Mademoiselle*. 53:236-9+. Ag. '61. Reprinted from *Mademoiselle*; © Street & Smith Publications, Inc., 1961.

concerns are more private than civic and, often, their revolts are nonpolitical—riots at Fort Lauderdale, panty raids, mass partying. Unlike students nearly everywhere else in the world, they are products of an educational system that is disengaged from social and political action.

What is significant now is the rise of a strong political minority—one that has restored action and political dialogue to the college campus. Action began first with the liberals. But lately a much publicized . . . response has come from the conservative students.

Adults who point happily to "unmistakable signs" of a conservative revolution in the colleges—the earmarks of a big switch to the Right—seem to have forgotten that there have always been conservative students on the college campus. (In the decades that followed Roosevelt and his New Deal, they simply went underground. They were quiescent. "Conservative" was a pejorative label then and no one wanted to be stuck with it.)

What *can* be said, however, with some accuracy, is that during the past year, conservative students have come to life. The new conservatives are not disinterested kids who maintain the status quo by political immobility, nor are they politically concerned but completely inactive sideliners. They form a bloc. They are unashamed, bold, and articulately enamored of certain doctrines: the sovereignty of individual self-interest; extremely limited government; a free-market economy; victory over, rather than coexistence with, the Communists, and so forth. These ideas are not new; most of them hark back to the era before Roosevelt. What is new about the new conservatives is their militant mood, their appearance on picket lines. . . .

The first spark of a new conservative movement appeared at the Republican convention in 1952: a group of young adults were . . . unable to reconcile themselves to the defeat of their candidate, Robert A. Taft. . . . Some members of the Taft group, now graduate students or young college teachers, are still influential on campus.

There was a second spark in 1953, when a handful of students formed the Intercollegiate Society of Individualists, hoping to educate other students about the virtues of conservative philosophy. (The ISI started with a mailing list of four hundred students. Now it boasts a list of thirteen thousand students and professors who have expressed interest in receiving *The Individualist,* a monthly newsletter.)

But even the launching in 1955 of William F. Buckley, Jr.'s *National Review,* a conservative weekly (which considers itself the opposite number of liberal news magazines like *The Nation* and *The New Republic*), was not enough to get a conservative movement off the ground.

Proof that there were actually a number of potentially conservative students ready to act did not turn up until two years ago when, to counter liberal students' protests against the loyalty oath required of students applying for funds made available by the National Defense Education Act, a pro-loyalty-oath petition was circulated in the East. Hundreds of signatures were gathered.

Shortly afterward, conservative students engaged in a more serious attempt to make their desires known: they organized the Youth for Goldwater movement, which upset so many of the Old Guard at the 1960 GOP convention. . . .

[John Weicher, a University of Chicago graduate student, claims that] from work at the convention, . . . a new conservative student, one with a "sense of reality," developed. A month later, at the Buckley family estate in Sharon, Connecticut, the "realistic conservatives" met, decided to throw their weight behind the new, action-oriented group, Young Americans for Freedom, and released the now-famous Sharon Statement, which outlines conservative beliefs.

John Weicher says, "Not all the kids who were at Sharon want to go into business, or to professional schools nor do I think they were all very selfish, though many were. Most of them are driven by a desire to be free to see what they can do in life without interference."

Yale law student, Robert Schuchman, YAF's national chairman, puts it this way: "We do not want to be told what we must do . . . we want to be self-determined."

It is obvious, however, that conservatives are not desperately concerned about the principle of self-determination when it is applied to other people besides themselves. Talking about the Peace Corps, for example, Schuchman says: "There are two questions. First, what face do we put on so as to get into these other countries? Clearly, humanitarian. Second, what is our real aim? Clearly, the promotion of our national interest against that of the Sino-Soviet bloc." The approving manner in which Schuchman presents the promotion of purely "national" interest must, one feels, offend many students who think the Peace Corps should not attempt to sell the United States abroad.

Not all young people to the right of center are overjoyed about the prominence of Barry Goldwater and the YAF. *Advance,* a liberal Republican journal, edited by Harvard students, characterizes YAF-ers as having a "cranky mentality" that deals in slogans rather than the solid fabric of logically connected ideas. *Advance* suspects that everything is not youthful and spontaneous about the student conservative movement. Many of the movement's leaders were long ago graduated from college and, as *Advance* puts it, "Just to help the grass roots sprout, YAF also hires full-time college organizers."

YAF's biggest spectacle so far was a mass rally . . . [in March 1961] in New York at which awards were presented to various leaders of American conservatism. Conservative students have also petitioned against the admission of Red China to the United Nations and demonstrated at the Connecticut submarine launching sites in sympathy with America's Polaris missile program. [They have demonstrated in support of HUAC and] they are hoping to tour Formosa in order to celebrate its integrity. For the most part, they do not involve themselves in what they have described as time-wasting campus or local issues. Actually, however, conservative programs are fewer than fanfare would have us believe. *Advance,* and other critics, have intimated that the YAF-ers seem to be geared more to creating a public image than to anything else. The conservatives' hypothesis seems to be: Given a conservative press, publicity, a superb public relations machine, and funds from wealthy adults, we can declare a "movement" and then fill it with people. . . .

YAF, the largest and most important of the young conservative organizations . . . estimates its membership at 24,000 students on over 115 campuses. A West Coast journalist points out in an article in *The Nation* that this would mean something like two hundred members per campus, and yet, Yale, which boasts a good-sized student body and YAF's national chairman, claims a membership of only seventy or eighty.

But if ability to make news, to swell membership rosters and mailing lists, is a strength of the young conservative movement, it is also a weakness. The young conservatives, one observer said, should stop trying to create an illusion, and, instead, concentrate on giving their movement content. American conservatives, as *National Review* editor Buckley has pointed out, have yet to come up with a conservative program that "speaks to our time." . . .

One wonders whether conservatism will continue to hold the interest of the young if it sticks to its present guns. These make a smart noise. But when the air clears and one reflects on what one has heard, it sounds to me more and more like: Me first, America second, and let the rest of the world go by.

Conservative students today feel alienated from the mainstream of political and intellectual America—alienated in a way that only liberals have felt in the past. The conservatives are weary of all that is liberal in our Establishment. And their dislike is strong enough to move them from lethargy to active concern. . . . Like the most militant of conservative students, the liberals, too, tend to be dissatisfied with the leadership of their elders—"adults don't *do* anything," is a frequent cry. Only a few members of the nonstudent left . . . and leaders of the nonviolence movement seem to have won their respect. Students expelled from southern colleges and jailed students are quoted regularly in liberal students' articles and political statements, but polished spokesmen, like Arthur Schlesinger, Jr., are totally ignored. . . .

Examples of the liberals' activity are numerous—some as familiar and notable as the student sit-ins and the Freedom Rides in the South, whose leaders couldn't wait any longer to win their rights through Federal action, the courts, or both; they found society unresponsive, so they undertook a struggle which by now is forcing the South, and the rest of the nation as well, perhaps, to make room for them by altering its laws, moralities, and customs. Students as far apart as Berkeley and Swarthmore are not waiting for the House of Representatives to abolish its Un-American Activities Committee; they are demonstrating against the committee wherever possible and distributing educational material, including records and tapes they have themselves transcribed. In the same way, the radical Student Peace Union is going ahead . . . on its program of demonstrations and educational activity in the cause of disarmament. And college students on the West Coast are working—without waiting for guidance from the American Congress—on improving living conditions for migrant laborers; . . . [in the summer of 1961] hundreds of them . . . [were] out in the California fields, talking up unionization as they . . . [worked] alongside the laborers. Finally, it was students who went to work immediately on raising supplies for the deprived communities of Negro sharecroppers in Fayette and Haywood counties in Tennessee—while the Justice Department worked at the slower process of improving conditions by legal means.

On at least one occasion, students found a channel receptive to their urgency: the Government-sponsored Peace Corps. But even the student Peace Corps movement, composed for the most part of extremely inexperienced and nonpolitical undergraduates, has to a great extent lost faith in the President and his administration. The reason: Cuba. After the Cuban invasion, students asked, how could America possibly tell Latin Americans it wanted to establish purely humanitarian Peace Corps units in their countries?

Liberal students protest that the United States is not practicing a moral alternative to undemocratic systems. America evidently has yet to learn that a country cannot educate its young to the ideas of freedom and human dignity, it cannot justify itself, without putting such principles into practice. When a country tries to have it both ways, there is resentment, frustration, and finally revolt. The liberal student is liberated from the McCarthy era, but he is still balked by a society that tolerates his voice but doesn't listen to it. . . .

Ideologies have in the past provided men with the assurances they needed to make all-or-nothing decisions; but . . . liberal students today are finding human affairs too complicated to be condensed in fixed, orderly systems. . . . A nonideological social movement has one clear advantage: it rejects the illusions and super-truths that in this century have licensed revolutionaries to use any means, often violent ones, to gain their ends. . . .

The absence of ideology, however, leaves a dangerous vacuum which too often is filled with emotionalism. "Students have a mystique about action," says Al Haber, president of the nation-wide Students for a Democratic Society (student branch of the venerable and liberal League for Industrial Democracy). "They are thrilled by action per se; the passion usually associated with ideology is transferred to the actual doing of the deed."

Haber, who has traveled to many campuses this year to establish new SDS groups, is critical of a lack of depth and clearly defined direction in student politics. Liberal students, he says, too rarely offer "an alternative beyond direct action. They call for disarmament, but say nothing of what to do with the manpower resources, industrial plant, and capital equipment that is tied up in the military machine. Problems of poverty, health care, wasted agricultural resources, meaningless work—these issues arouse students neither to demonstration nor discussion."

The activities of the past few years, Haber says, have marked a first step "away from social irresponsibility." But in the future, liberals must "evolve radical alternatives to the inadequate society of today and . . . develop . . . a communication system that will give perspective to immediate actions."

The liberals at present lack such a unifying organization. . . .

Partly because the student liberal movement *is* disconnected and uncoordinated, many of its members have only a shallow understanding of issues. Unless the liberals set up a framework, the movement could go in either of two directions:

It could continue on in shallowness, responding sporadically when a sense of "mission" is felt.

It could end in a return to privatism on the campuses. Mere excitement surrounding political action does not guarantee a stable, long-range (indeed one hopes, lifetime) program of social action and criticism.

One indication that liberal students do want substance as well as slogans is the recent appearance of several small magazines and newsletters concerned with political and social problems. They are mostly mimeo-and-staple affairs: the *Albatross* at Swarthmore, which solicits letters from students (they may submit copies of letters they have written to congressmen or editors); *The Activist* at Oberlin, which recently switched its editorial line from news of demonstrations to a more varied, thoughtful content; *Controversy* and *Dialogue* at Cornell; *New*

University Thought at Chicago. These publications are analytical—groping for a more complete theoretical foundation for student action....

Some students are organizing their energies through the creation of campus political parties, which attack both local and national issues, and sponsor candidates for student government. Slate, at Berkeley, . . . helped activate parties all along the West Coast. The Progressive Student League at Oberlin has helped set up parties at Macalester, Trenton State, Fenn, Notre Dame, Wayne State, and the universities of Wisconsin, Minnesota, Pennsylvania, and Rochester. Voice is active at Michigan, Polit at Chicago—virtually none of these groups existed two years ago.

Liberals have achieved some impressive results so far: in the integration struggle, in the formation of the Peace Corps, in the attack on HUAC....

This last year, however, has seen a lot of dropouts among students who were in the liberal movement just for thrills. "There will never be another spring 1960," says an integrationist in Atlanta. "There is less glory now, and more and more daily plugging." What he says applies not only to southern campuses but also to many civil rights groups that sprang up on northern campuses to support the sit-ins and that are turning from picket lines to grinding work on complex, local problems. (EPIC, the Emergency Public Integration Committee formed by colleges around Boston, is taking up questions of fair housing for Negroes and other minority groups in the area.)

If the chaos of liberal action today is ever going to evolve into a valid social movement, students must continue to supplement excitement with hard work, moral protest with political articulateness, spontaneous demonstrations with undramatic hours spent at political education.

A PERMANENT PEACE CORPS [5]

I recommend to the Congress the establishment of a permanent Peace Corps—a pool of trained American men and women

[5] From message delivered by President John F. Kennedy to the House of Representatives on March 1, 1961. (H. Doc. no 98) United States. House of Representatives. 87th Congress, 1st session. Supt. of Docs. Washington 25, D.C. '61. p 2733-4.

sent overseas by the United States Government or through private organizations and institutions to help foreign countries meet their urgent needs for skilled manpower.

I have today signed an Executive Order establishing a Peace Corps on a temporary pilot basis.

The temporary Peace Corps will be a source of information and experience to aid us in formulating more effective plans for a permanent organization. . . . This temporary Peace Corps is being established under existing authority in the Mutual Security Act and will be located in the Department of State. Its initial expenses will be paid from appropriations currently available for our foreign aid program.

Throughout the world the people of the newly developing nations are struggling for economic and social progress which reflects their deepest desires. Our own freedom, and the future of freedom around the world, depend, in a very real sense, on their ability to build growing and independent nations where men can live in dignity, liberated from the bonds of hunger, ignorance, and poverty.

One of the greatest obstacles to the achievement of this goal is the lack of trained men and women with the skill to teach the young and assist in the operation of development projects—men and women with the capacity to cope with the demands of swiftly evolving economies, and with the dedication to put that capacity to work in the villages, the mountains, the towns and the factories of dozens of struggling nations.

The vast task of economic development urgently requires skilled people to do the work of the society—to help teach in the schools, construct development projects, demonstrate modern methods of sanitation in the villages, and perform a hundred other tasks calling for training and advanced knowledge.

To meet this urgent need for skilled manpower we are proposing the establishment of a Peace Corps—an organization which will recruit and train American volunteers, sending them abroad to work with the people of other nations.

This organization will differ from existing assistance programs in that its members will supplement technical advisers by offering the specific skills needed by developing nations if they are to put technical advice to work. They will help provide the skilled manpower necessary to carry out the development projects planned by the host governments, acting at a working level and serving at great personal sacrifice. There is little doubt that the number of those who wish to serve will be far greater than our capacity to absorb them.

The Peace Corps or some similar approach has been strongly advocated by Senator [Hubert H.] Humphrey [Democrat of Minnesota], Representative [Henry S.] Reuss [Democrat of Wisconsin] and others in Congress. It has received strong support from universities, voluntary agencies, student groups, labor unions, and business and professional organizations.

Last session the Congress authorized a study of these possibilities. Preliminary reports of this study show that the Peace Corps is feasible, needed and wanted by many foreign countries.

Most heartening of all, the initial reaction to this proposal has been an enthusiastic response by student groups, professional organizations and private citizens everywhere—a convincing demonstration that we have in this country an immense reservoir of dedicated men and women willing to devote their energies and time and toil to the cause of world peace and human progress.

Among the specific programs to which Peace Corps members can contribute are: teaching in primary and secondary schools, especially as part of national English-language teaching programs; participation in the world-wide program of malaria eradication; instruction and operation of public health and sanitation projects; aiding in village development through school construction and other programs; increasing rural agricultural productivity by assisting local farmers to use modern implements and techniques. The initial emphasis of these programs will be on teaching. Thus the Peace Corps members will be an effective means of implementing the development programs of the host countries—programs which our technical assistance operations have helped to formulate.

The Peace Corps will not be limited to the young, or to college graduates. All Americans who are qualified will be welcome to join this effort. But undoubtedly the corps will be made up primarily of young people as they complete their formal education.

Because one of the greatest resources of a free society is the strength and diversity of its private organizations and institutions much of the Peace Corps program will be carried out by these groups, financially assisted by the Federal Government.

Sources of Supply

Peace Corps personnel will be made available to developing nations in the following ways:

1. Through private voluntary agencies carrying on international assistance programs.
2. Through overseas programs of colleges and universities.
3. Through assistance programs of international agencies.
4. Through assistance programs of the United States Government.
5. Through new programs which the Peace Corps itself directly administers.

In the majority of cases the Peace Corps will assume the entire responsibility for recruitment, training and the development of overseas projects. In other cases it will make available a pool of trained applicants to private groups who are carrying out the projects approved by the Peace Corps.

In the case of Peace Corps programs conducted through voluntary agencies and universities, these private institutions will have the option of using the national recruitment system—the central pool of trained manpower—or developing recruitment systems of their own.

In all cases men and women recruited as a result of Federal assistance will be members of the Peace Corps and enrolled in the central organization. All private recruitment and training programs will adhere to Peace Corps standards as a condition of Federal assistance.

In all instances the men and women of the Peace Corps will go only to those countries where their services and skills are genuinely needed and desired. United States operations missions, supplemented where necessary by special Peace Corps teams, will consult with leaders in foreign countries in order to determine where Peace Corpsmen are needed, the types of job they can best fill, and the number of people who can be usefully employed. The Peace Corps will not supply personnel for marginal undertakings without a sound economic or social justification. In furnishing assistance through the Peace Corps careful regard will be given to the particular country's developmental priorities.

Membership in the Peace Corps will be open to all Americans, and applications will be available shortly. Where application is made directly to the Peace Corps—the vast majority of cases—they will be carefully screened to make sure that those who are selected can contribute to Peace Corps programs, and have the personal qualities which will enable them to represent the United States abroad with honor and dignity. In those cases where application is made directly to a private group, the same basic standards will be maintained. Each new recruit will receive a training and orientation period varying from six weeks to six months. This training will include courses in the culture and language of the country to which they are being sent and specialized training designed to increase the work skills of recruits. In some cases training will be conducted by participant agencies and universities in approved training programs. Other training programs will be conducted by the Peace Corps staff.

Length of service in the corps will vary depending on the kind of project and the country, generally ranging from two to three years. Peace Corps members will often serve under conditions of physical hardship, living under primitive conditions among the people of developing nations. For every Peace Corps member service will mean a great financial sacrifice. They will receive no salary. Instead they will be given an allowance which will only be sufficient to meet their basic needs and maintain health. It is essential that Peace Corpsmen and women live simply and unostentatiously among the people they have come to assist. At the conclusion of their tours, members of the Peace Corps will receive a small sum in the form of severance pay based on length of service abroad, to assist them during their first weeks back in the United States. Service with the Peace Corps will not exempt volunteers from Selective Service.

The United States will assume responsibility for supplying medical services to Peace Corps members and ensuring supplies and drugs necessary to good health.

I have asked the temporary Peace Corps to begin plans and make arrangements for pilot programs. A minimum of several hundred volunteers could be selected, trained and at work abroad by the end of this calendar year. It is hoped that within a few years several thousand Peace Corps members will be working in foreign lands.

It is important to remember that this program must, in its early stages, be experimental in nature. This is a new dimension in our overseas program and only the most careful planning and negotiation can insure its success.

The benefits of the Peace Corps will not be limited to the countries in which it serves. Our own young men and women will be enriched by the experience of living and working in foreign lands. They will have acquired new skills and experience which will aid them in their future careers and add to our own country's supply of trained personnel and teachers. They will return better able to assume the responsibilities of American citizenship and with greater understanding of our global responsibilities.

Although this is an American Peace Corps, the problem of world development is not just an American problem. Let us hope that other nations will mobilize the spirit and energies and skill of their people in some form of Peace Corps—making our own effort only one step in a major international effort to increase the welfare of all men and improve understanding among nations.

AN ABC OF THE PEACE CORPS [6]

The Peace Corps has already ignited more public enthusiasm than any other program sponsored by the new Administration. But there are worriers and critics as well.

The Peace Corps was established by President Kennedy by executive order . . . [on March 1, 1961] on a "temporary pilot basis." The President also sent a message to Congress requesting

[6] From article by Peter Braestrup, New York *Times* correspondent. New York *Times*. p E8. Mr. 12, '61. Reprinted by permission.

legislation to make the Corps permanent. [Legislation establishing the Corps as a permanent agency of the Federal Government was passed by Congress and signed by the President in September 1961.—Ed.]

The idea is to send abroad by year's end some five hundred to one thousand trained American men and women to help other nations "meet their urgent need for skilled manpower." . . .

R. Sargent Shriver, forty-five, former president of the Chicago Board of Education and Mr. Kennedy's brother-in-law, was named director of the Corps. Mr. Shriver had headed the Administration's Peace Corps planning since January [1961] and it was he who urged the President to get it started without further delay. He is serving without salary. . . .

What follows is a brief run-down of how the Peace Corps will operate:

Financing: Initial financing of the program through the end of June will come through already appropriated Mutual Security funds. For the following fiscal years, special appropriations will be required from Congress. The cost per overseas worker per year is estimated by Peace Corps officials at between $10,000 and $12,000—including training, transportation, living allowances, medical care and administrative overhead.

Thus, with two thousand workers overseas, the annual cost would run between $20 and $24 million, a relatively modest slice of the $80 billion Federal budget. [Congress appropriated $30 million for the Peace Corps' first year of operation.—Ed.]

Purpose: Peace Corps volunteers of both sexes would operate as teachers or as "technicians' helpers" in the fields of education, agriculture, public health, English language instruction, urban renewal, public administration. The initial emphasis will be on teaching. The volunteers will work only in projects which, by Peace Corps standards, "will make a difference." They will operate only at the invitation of the host countries and they will work largely under their authority.

The volunteers, as Peace Corps officials see them, will essentially fill the gap between the present technical advisers and local experts on the one hand and relatively unskilled local labor on the other. The object, an official said, "is not to have the volunteers do what native manpower can do on its own."

Organization: The corps will be a semiautonomous agency under the State Department. Peace Corps volunteers will also work in approved programs undertaken by private universities, voluntary private agencies, the ICA [International Cooperation Administration], and United Nations bodies. Overseas a small number of Peace Corps liaison officers will provide administrative support. . . .

Peace Corps officials say that people with trade skills—in construction or home economics, for example—are just as welcome as those with college degrees. The minimum age requirement is eighteen. But the vast majority of those accepted is expected to come from the twenty-two to thirty-five age group.

Screening: Peace Corps officials stress that applicants will be thoroughly screened for emotional stability, work skills and intelligence. The idea will be to fit the volunteer to projects already slated. Screening procedures will include an FBI security check, written tests and a battery of interviews.

Training: Training will begin on a dozen campuses in June. Later Peace Corps Staff Centers and overseas training stations will also be set up. Each recruit will go through . . . months of rigorous language training, foreign culture courses and occupational training. The training period will also serve as a further screening period. If the recruit does not measure up he will quietly be dropped. . . .

Life Overseas: Depending on his assignment, the Peace Corps volunteer will spend two to three years overseas. He will get only a basic allowance sufficient to match local living standards. For example, if he is a teacher he will get enough money to live as do the local teachers.

Peace Corps officials say that great care will be taken to insure that the volunteers work under experienced supervision. Technician helpers, for example, will work under ICA technical advisers. They will follow up, say, a demonstration to villagers on how to control malaria, by staying in the area, mapping the mosquito-infested marshes and doing the fairly simple field testing required.

Use for Other Agencies: Administration policy will prohibit any use of the Peace Corps for religious missionary purposes, or by the Central Intelligence Agency. The program is not designed as a propaganda operation or as a means of spreading American influence on the local political scene.

Legal Restrictions: Peace Corps volunteers will come under treaties now governing court jurisdiction over ICA personnel overseas. Some countries give ICA people diplomatic immunity. Some do not. In any event, Mr. Shriver has said that bad actors will be uncovered as soon as possible. In case of doubt, the volunteer will be shipped home. Some Peace Corps officials point to the successful experience of private agencies overseas. Very few incidents have occurred, and none of them have been serious enough to shake world opinion.

Discharge Procedure: After his overseas tour, the volunteer will get travel expenses home, and an accumulated "bonus" of $50 to $75 for each month of overseas service. In addition, a Peace Corps career board will develop job opportunities for its veterans.

Draft Status: Although there will be no automatic draft exemption for Peace Corps duty, General Lewis B. Hershey, Selective Service Director, has stated that barring some national crisis the corpsmen would probably be able to get indefinite deferments—de facto exemption—if they work in some occupation "in the national interest." These occupations would presumably include government service or teaching.

PEACE CORPS FINDS IT IS IN DEMAND[7]

In his State of the Union message . . . [on January 11, 1962], President Kennedy proudly hailed a bright light on the no-longer New Frontier:

> The newly conceived Peace Corps is winning friends and helping people in fourteen countries—supplying trained and dedicated young men and women to give them a hand in building a society and a glimpse of American idealism. If there is a problem here, it is that we cannot supply the spontaneous and mounting demand [for volunteers overseas]. . . .

This is a far cry from last spring when R. Sargent Shriver, the agency's director, set forth on a round-the-world trip, with

[7] From article by Peter Braestrup, New York *Times* correspondent. New York *Times*. p E5. Ja. 14, '62. Reprinted by permission.

some inner misgivings, "to test the market" for person-to-person projects. Today, in the teacher category alone, the Peace Corps has requests from thirty-six countries for some 4,000 qualified volunteers.

[On January 7, 1962] Mr. Shriver called for 800 more volunteers to meet demands from eleven countries—enough manpower to double the corps' present enrollment. By July 1, the corps' strength will go over 2,000.

The statistics change every day. This is . . . [the] score-card [as of January 1962]:

Overseas are 654 volunteers; in training are 104 more, and about to go to Thailand are 45 others. The volunteers overseas are working in Chile, Colombia, Ghana, Nigeria, Pakistan, the Philippines, St. Lucia, Tanganyika, India, Sierra Leone and Malaya. In training this month are groups destined for El Salvador and Brazil.

The eleven newly announced projects, requiring some 800 volunteers, are for Tunisia, Ethiopia, the Ivory Coast, Somalia, Honduras, Togo, Jamaica, North Borneo and Sarawak, Venezuela, Bolivia and Peru. . . .

Experience, inevitably, has uncovered problems and necessitated some pragmatic changes in approach. . . .

Projects: Originally, Mr. Shriver guessed that a major share of the Peace Corps effort would go into two types of assistance, among others: malaria control and civil administration. However, foreign nations showed little interest in these fields. Predicted demands for teachers and for agricultural workers turned out to be far stronger. Two thirds of the first 750 volunteers are teachers of a variety of vocational and academic subjects. Now a broader variety of technical health and crafts projects is planned.

Recruiting: Back in March, the Peace Corps necessarily had to get going on specific projects to provide an initial focus for its recruiting-selection-training effort. Lead time was short, both because of the host country schedules, and the corps' desire to tap the June crop of college graduates. This caused some pains. . . .

The applicants pool, now some 15,000 strong, narrowed down for various causes to about 10 per cent, ready, available, and qualified for training on a given date. The biggest single segment is still made up of liberal arts graduates without special skills. These were trained as teachers. The corps had to stretch to get some of its specialists. . . .

The corps has recently turned to matching future projects to the skills available in the pool, rather than vice versa. This increases each applicant's chances. One thousand applications a month are currently coming in.

Training: The Peace Corps has used universities and colleges extensively as trainers of volunteers. A heavy share of its $30 million first-year budget has been earmarked for high-quality instruction.

However, the corps learned by harsh experience that (1) university lecturers were often ill-equipped to meet the down-to-earth needs of volunteers going off to strange lands; (2) some of the larger universities viewed the Peace Corps largely as a source of guinea pigs for research or of another nice Federal grant; (3) far more language instruction was required; (4) far more Peace Corps control and indoctrination was needed.

Private Agencies: Last June Mr. Shriver estimated that some eighteen projects might be handled by private overseas agencies by mid-1962. To date, four projects have been contracted out to such agencies. Two or three more are under negotiation. Perhaps a dozen in all may be agreed on by next year.

The difficulties have come largely over the disparities between the Government-run Peace Corps and the agencies' style of operation. For one thing, the Peace Corps likes to deal in fifty- to seventy-volunteer contingents, much larger than those handled by most private groups. The touchy church-state problem has so far shut out all sectarian agencies. The Peace Corps has not altered its church-state stand, but its officials are a good deal less optimistic on the chances of getting religious groups to run nonreligious Peace Corps projects.

These have been the chief areas of difficulty. One of the reasons none of the problems has crippled the corps is that Mr. Shriver has encouraged candor and debate, as well as long hours, among his 250-man staff. Matured as it is, the corps has yet to take on the bureaucratic trappings of older Federal agencies. This is perhaps its most precious asset, aside from the vigor of its leadership, in Washington. . . .

In the meantime, Mr. Shriver plans to [go] up to Capitol Hill . . . [in February 1962] to start wooing Congressional support for a second-year budget of something over $50 million and a modest increase of Peace Corps strength to 4,500 volunteers by mid-1963. His personal lobbying effort won the corps a lop-sided vote last year. As even top Republicans say privately, he will face less opposition . . . [in 1962].

A FORCE OF YOUTH AS A FORCE FOR PEACE [8]

Of all the campaign statements by President Kennedy, . . . his Peace Corps proposal, made . . . [in] November [1960] at San Francisco, more than any other reached directly into the hearts and minds of thousands of young men and women throughout the country. Clearly, it articulated a longing and a question that have been spreading for some time among many groups, both young and old: How can the individual American do something positive and affirmative for peace? . . .

Nearly half the world lives in grinding poverty—on a per capita income of about $100 a year, compared with $2,166 a year in the United States. Two thirds of the world is illiterate, compared with 98 per cent of Americans who can read and write. Life expectancy, because of such diseases as malaria and tuberculosis, is thirty-six years in the poorer areas, compared with almost seventy years in America.

Vast amounts of money have been poured into these areas, unilaterally and through the United Nations, to help people, shattered by war or poverty, to leapfrog the centuries and develop a better life.

Yet all these efforts have proved unequal to the astronomical need. Reports from congressional, United Nations and private sources indicate that the demand is for many times the number of people and projects. One congressman estimated after touring Asia that ten times the number of International Cooperation Administration specialists—or a total of sixty thousand men—could well be used on farm development projects alone.

Just as crucial as the manpower problem is the psychological factor. Americans serving abroad are chiefly ICA consultants

[8] From article by Gertrude Samuels, New York *Times* correspondent. New York *Times Magazine*. p 26. F. 5, '61. Reprinted by permission.

to governments—well-paid specialists who work in the capitals and rarely meet the people. Native peoples in many areas have the idea that America is the inheritor of the colonial tradition, that Americans like to keep on a plane of superiority far from them. Thus foreign aid has fallen short, the experts say, because it has been insufficiently human and understandable; it has relied too much on military hardware and on steel and concrete projects that may be necessary for defense and development but, by themselves, cannot make friends for us. . . .

The human picture of what is possible with a Peace Corps is glimpsed in the work of the major private agencies. Although they have only been able to scratch the surface of the problem, young Americans, volunteering for work with the agencies, have already been putting their idealism into practice in many countries.

The American Friends Service Committee (Quakers) sends some five hundred young Americans abroad during the summer vacation to help rebuild villages and schools. The International Voluntary Service (IVS), supported by the major world missionary groups, uses about 150 young Americans on a year-round basis.

Perhaps the best-known experiment, now in its third year, is Operation Crossroads Africa, organized by Dr. James H. Robinson, Negro pastor, and director of the Morningside Community Center of New York.

In 1954, Dr. Robinson toured Africa and saw the urgent needs of the villages. Back home, he failed to interest anyone in his person-to-person approach ("Everyone thought the idea was crazy") until he got to Occidental College in Los Angeles; nine hundred students there pitched in to initiate plans to send ten students with him to spend the summer of 1958 helping Africans.

As the idea spread to other campuses, Dr. Robinson received 270 applications; he chose sixty out of the group, of whom seventeen were Negroes. They understood that this was neither a tourist joy ride nor an African safari, but a tough, work-camp mission in which they would live simply, travel hard, and be willing to accept the risks of malaria, dysentery, and the primitive conditions of village life where few tourists or diplomats penetrate. Money for the project was raised by churches and civic groups, or contributed by the students themselves.

That first group, loaded with tropical medicine chests and zeal, went to impoverished villages in Liberia, Ghana, Nigeria, Sierra Leone, and the French Cameroons (now the Republic of Cameroon), where they were joined by African students. Practically every night there was an exchange of views about the United States and its role in Africa. "Always" there was the question of race relations.

The Americans were shocked at first to find that in many communities the educated elite scorned manual labor; African students would look on with amusement as Americans—boys and girls, Negro and white—went to work for their village. Finally, they were shamed into action and, as they began to work alongside the Americans, the illiterate villagers saw from the joint action that it was not undignified for the educated to work with their hands—"Work, it's okay," they said—and they, too, pitched in.

That summer, the Americans helped build a village water supply in the bush country of Gbendembu in Sierra Leone; a two-room, concrete block school and a stone chapel in the village of Buel in the French Cameroons; a seven-room school in a remote Ghanaian village. After working hours, they taught children elementary English, arithmetic, history and geography; the girls met with women's groups to teach homemaking and hygiene.

Since 1958, Operation Crossroads Africa has grown to a project of 180 students, chosen from 700 applicants from Harvard, Yale, MIT, Howard University and seventy other colleges. The students divide into teams of fifteen to twenty, assigned to ten West African countries. Most students are white, some two dozen are from southern states; almost half are women.

Last summer in the Sanniquelle District of Liberia, a team of Americans and one Canadian helped to build a library with materials from American firms in the country, working alongside African students from the University of Liberia. Sonja Bolling, twenty-year-old junior of Howard University, taught school after the manual labor—mathematics and spelling to a class of thirty-five who ranged in age from nine to eighteen years.

At Prampram, a fishing village on the Ghana coast, fourteen American students joined thirty Ghanaian students in building a schoolhouse. They had no modern amenities; they brought water by bucket from the village well; they managed on gas lamps, cooked their own meals (mainly meat stews with tropical yams and rice), and experienced one case of malaria. The blue-jeaned girls soon learned it was easier to carry mortar pans and concrete blocks on their heads; at lunch Americans and Africans shared coconuts and ideas for a better life.

The young Americans found they were not only creating a positive attitude for America but also acquiring educations themselves in foreign beliefs and social customs.

BIBLIOGRAPHY

An asterisk (*) preceding a reference indicates that the article or a part of it has been reprinted in this book.

I. EDUCATION

Bibliographies

United States. Department of Health, Education and Welfare. Office of Education. Scholarships and fellowships: a selected bibliography. The Office. Washington 25, D.C. '57.

United States. Department of Health, Education and Welfare. Office of Education. Student financial aid in higher education: an annotated bibliography. The Office. Washington 25, D.C. '61.

Books and Pamphlets

American Legion. Education and Scholarship Program. National Child Welfare Division. Need a lift? 11th ed. The Program. Box 1055. Indianapolis 6. '61.

American Library Association. Library Education Division. Fellowships, scholarships, grants-in-aid, loan funds and other assistance for library education in the United States and Canada. The Association. 50 E. Huron St. Chicago 11. '61.

*B'nai B'rith Vocational Service Bureau. Careers for technical school graduates. The Bureau. 1424 16th St. N.W. Washington 6, D.C. '52.

Boroff, David. Campus U.S.A.; portraits of American colleges in action. Harper. New York. '61.

Bowles, F. H. How to get into college. Dutton. New York. '58.

Carnegie Corporation of New York. Annual report. New York. '60.
From high school to job. p 11-20.

Cohen, N. M. ed. Vocational training directory of the United States. 3d ed. Potomac Press. Arlington 1, Va. '58.

Conant, J. B. Slums and suburbs: a commentary on schools in metropolitan areas. McGraw. New York. '61.

Council on Social Work Education. Fellowships and scholarships in the United States and Canada. The Council. 345 E. 46th St. New York 17. '61.

Croner, U. H. E. comp. American trade schools directory, 1957-58. Croner Publications. 211-13 Jamaica Ave. Queens Village, N.Y. '57.

Daniels, W. M. ed. Educational opportunities for youth. (Reference Shelf v 27, no 5) Wilson. New York. '55.

Engineers' Council for Professional Development. Accredited technical school programs. The Council. 345 E. 47th St. New York 17. '61.

Feingold, S. N. Scholarships, fellowships and loans. 4v. Bellman. Cambridge, Mass. '49-61.

Fine, Benjamin. How to be accepted by the college of your choice. Channel Press. New York. '60.

Gleazer, E. J. Jr. American junior colleges. National Council on Education. 1785 Massachusetts Ave. N.W. Washington 6, D.C. '60.

Hawes, G. R. New American guide to colleges. New American Library. New York. '59.

Institute of International Education. Foreign study for undergraduates. The Institute. 800 Second Ave. New York 17. '58.

Institute of International Education. Group study abroad. The Institute. 800 Second Ave. New York 17. '61.

Institute of International Education. Handbook on international study: for U.S. nationals. The Institute. 800 Second Ave. New York 17. '61.

Institute of International Education. International exchange programs for teen-agers. The Institute. 800 Second Ave. New York 17. '61.

Institute of International Education. Summer study abroad. The Institute. 800 Second Ave. New York 17. '62.

Irwin, Mary, ed. American universities and colleges. 5th ed. American Council on Education. 1785 Massachusetts Ave. N.W. Washington 6, D.C. '60.

Kinkead, K. T. How an ivy league college decides on admissions. Norton. New York. '61.

Expanded from: New Yorker. 36:132-6+. S. 10, '60. Reporter at large; selecting the freshman class at Yale.

*Klein, Jerry and Fisher, Bill. So you didn't go to college. (Public Affairs Pamphlet no 249) Public Affairs Committee. 22 E. 38th St. New York 16. '57.

Layton, W. K. Special services for the drop-out and the potential drop-out. National Committee on Employment of Youth. 419 Park Ave. S. New York 19. '52.

Lovejoy, C. E. Lovejoy's college guide. Simon & Schuster. New York. '59.

Lovejoy, C. E. Lovejoy's vocational school guide; a handbook of job training opportunities. Simon & Schuster. New York. '55.

Lovejoy, C. E. and Jones, T. S. Lovejoy-Jones college scholarship guide. Simon & Schuster. New York. '57.

McClellan, G. S. ed. America's educational needs. (Reference Shelf v 30, no 5) Wilson. New York. '58.

Mattingly, R. C. Financial aid for college students: graduate. United States. Department of Health, Education and Welfare. Office of Education. Washington 25, D.C. '57.

*National Education Association. Department of Classroom Teachers and Research Division. High school dropouts. The Association. 1201 16th St. N.W. Washington 6, D.C. '59.

National University Extension Association. Guide to correspondence study. The Association. University of Minnesota. Minneapolis. '60.

Sargent, P. E. Junior colleges, specialized schools and colleges. Sargent. Boston. '59.

Shepard, D. A. Liberal education in an industrial society. (Public Affairs Pamphlet no 248) Public Affairs Committee. 22 E. 38th St. New York 16. '57.

United Nations Educational, Scientific, and Cultural Organization. Study Abroad 1961-62. v 13. UNESCO Publications Center, 801 Third Ave. New York 22. '61.
Annual.

United States. Department of Health, Education and Welfare. Office of Education. National Defense Student Loan Program, including participating institutions. The Office. Washington 25, D.C. '60.

Vocational Advisory Service. Where to find vocational training in New York City. The Service. 432 Fourth Ave. New York 16. '58.

Wilkins, T. B. Financial aid for college students: undergraduate. United States. Department of Health, Education and Welfare. Office of Education. Washington 25, D.C. '57.

Periodicals

American Child (National Committee on Employment of Youth). 42:1-24. My. '60. Apprenticeship.

American Child (National Committee on Employment of Youth). 43:1-19. Mr. '61. Dropouts: number one challenge to America's schools.

Annals of the American Academy of Political and Social Science. 335:1-165. My. '61. Rising demand for international education; ed. by J. F. Melby [entire issue].

Better Homes and Gardens. 38:102+. S. '60. When choosing a college don't fall for these fables. Gordon Greer.

*Better Homes and Gardens. 38:106+. O. '60. How not to pick a college haphazardly. Gordon Greer.

Changing Times. 13:15-17. Jl. '59. College costs for married students.

Changing Times. 14:25-8. Mr. '60. Straight talk about scholarships.

Changing Times. 14:22-5. Jl. '60. Can you work your way through college?

*Changing Times. 14:41-4. S. '60. How to pay for college.

*Changing Times. 15:36-9. Jl. '61. It doesn't have to be a regular four-year college.

Editorial Research Reports. 2:705-22. S. 25, '57. Liberal education. Martin Packman.

Harper's Magazine. 216:49-54. F. '58. How to choose a college, if any. J. W. Gardner.

Ladies' Home Journal. 76:64-5+. O. '59. Is college education a right or a privilege?

Ladies' Home Journal. 77:30+. My. '60. Public concern for all American youth. J. B. Conant.

Look. 24:26-8+. D. 6, '60. Who should go to a junior college?
Mademoiselle. 50:84-7+. Ja. '60. How to discover a college. Paul Woodring.
National Education Association Journal. 50:16-18. F. '61. Vocational education. R. C. Wenrich.
National Education Association Journal. 50:27-9. F. '61. Maturing of the junior college. Erwin Knoll.
New York Times. p 53. Jl. 23, '61. Los Angeles aids adult schooling. Bill Becker.
New York Times. p E9. S. 10, '61. New college tide. F. M. Hechinger.
New York Times. p 56. S. 24, '61. Disabled students. H. A. Rusk.
New York Times Magazine. p 11+. F. 14, '60. American fetish, the college degree. David Boroff.
New York Times Magazine. p 23+. My. 7, '61. Huge waste: educated womanpower. M. I. Bunting.
Newsweek. 58:94+. O. 23, '61. Women of talent.
Saturday Evening Post. 228:42-3+. N. 19, '55. How to choose a college. C. E. Lovejoy (as told to Jerome Ellison).
Saturday Evening Post. 233:31+. N. 12, '60. Why we turn them down. E. T. Chamberlain, Jr.
Saturday Review. 44:56-7. F. 18, '61. Wayfaring scholars. H. S. Commager.
Saturday Review. 44:58-9+. F. 18, '61. World is their campus. J. F. Fixx.
School and Society. 88:399-400. O. 22, '60. Study of cooperative education. J. W. Wilson.
*School and Society. 88:446-7. N. 19, '60. Admission policy in state-supported higher education. R. G. Lloyd.
School and Society. 89:86-7. F. 25, '61. Scholarships for junior college transfer students. R. E. Schultz.
Senior Scholastic. 69:7-9. D. 6, '56. School days for how many years?
Senior Scholastic. 78:8-9. F. 8, '61. "Right" college, or the right college for you? C. D. O'Connell.
U.S. News & World Report. 48:78-83. F. 1, '60. How you now can finance a college education; interview with J. F. Morse.
U.S. News & World Report. 48:70-3. Mr. 28, '60. How to tell who should go to college; interview with F. H. Bowles.
U.S. News & World Report. 50:70-8. F. 27, '61. If you're choosing a college: facts a survey turns up.

II. EMPLOYMENT

Books and Pamphlets

It's your choice: how to choose the military service program that will serve you best. It's Your Choice. Washington 25, D.C. '60.
*Killingsworth, C. C. Effects of automation on employment and manpower planning. (1960-61 Reprint Series no 37) Labor and Industrial Relations Center. Michigan State University. East Lansing. '60.

National Association of Manufacturers. Your opportunities in industry as a skilled craftsman. The Association. 2 E. 48th St. New York 17. '59.

National Association of Manufacturers. Your opportunities in industry as a technician. The Association. 2 E. 48th St. New York 17. '57.

New York Life Insurance Company. Career opportunities. The Company. 51 Madison Ave. New York 10. '58.

New York State. Department of Labor. Division of Employment. From campus to career: a guide for generalists. The Division. 500 Eighth Ave. New York 18. '60.

*Robinson, H. A. You and your career. Library and Educational Division. Crowell-Collier. 640 Fifth Ave. New York 19. '61.

United States. Department of Health, Education and Welfare. Children's Bureau. Some facts for young workers about work and labor laws. Supt. of Docs. Washington 25, D.C. '59.

United States. Department of Labor. Choosing your occupation. Supt. of Docs. Washington 25, D.C. '60.

United States. Department of Labor. Fact sheet on youth entering the labor force. The Department. Washington 25, D.C. '60.

United States. Department of Labor. Job guide for young workers. Supt. of Docs. Washington 25, D.C. '60.

United States. Department of Labor. Open letter to the college graduates of 1961 from Secretary of Labor Arthur J. Goldberg. The Department. Washington 25, D.C. '61.

United States. Department of Labor. Summer jobs for students. Supt. of Docs. Washington 25, D.C. '60.

United States. Department of Labor. Bureau of Labor Statistics. From school to work. The Bureau. Washington 25, D.C. '60.

United States. Department of Labor. Bureau of Labor Statistics. Occupational outlook handbook. Supt. of Docs. Washington 25, D.C. '61.

United States. Department of Labor. Women's Bureau. Future jobs for high school girls. (Women's Bureau Pamphlet no 7) The Bureau. Washington 25, D.C. '59.

United States. Department of Labor. Women's Bureau. Job horizons for the college woman. (Women's Bureau Pamphlet no 1) The Bureau. Washington 25, D.C. '56.

Periodicals

American Child (National Committee on Employment of Youth). 41:1-20. N. '59. Industry programs for youth.

*American Child (National Committee on Employment of Youth). 42:1-24. Mr. '60. Automation and youth; forecasts by Walter Reuther and others.

Reprinted in this book: Investment in the future. J. M. Rosow.

American Child (National Committee on Employment of Youth). 42: 1-19. N. '60. Job help for youth in the sixties.

Business Week. p 56. Ag. 5, '61. New business ways in the South.

Changing Times. 13:15-17. Je. '59. Jobs for high school graduates.

Commonweal. 73:606-8. Mr. 10, '61. Negroes at work. T. R. Brooks.

Editorial Research Reports. 2:105-21. F. 13, '57. Woman's place in the economy. H. B. Shaffer.

*Editorial Research Reports. 11:501-17. Jl. 12, '61. Jobs for young people. H. B. Shaffer.

Editorial Research Reports. 11:574-90. Ag. 5, '61. Negro employment. H. B. Shaffer.

*Harvard Business Review. 35:65-74. Ja.-F. '57. American Negroes—a wasted resource. J. J. Morrow.

Industrial Arts and Vocational Education. 49:50+. F. '60. Employment prospects for youth in the 1960's. Elaine Exton.

Industrial Arts and Vocational Education. 49:18-19+. N. '60. Our critical craftsmen shortage. E. K. Hankin.

Mademoiselle. 51:49-55. Je. '60. Twenty-four jobs, or what can you do with a B.A.?

Monthly Labor Review. 83:952-7. S. '60. Negroes in apprenticeship; New York State.

New York Times. p E10. Ap. 23, '61. Jobs: where will new ones be? A. H. Raskin.

New York Times Magazine. p 15-16. Je. 9, '57. Promise and peril of automation. D. A. Morse.

New York Times Magazine. p 11+. Ap. 2, '61. Challenge of "industrial revolution II." A. J. Goldberg.

Occupational Outlook Quarterly. 4:10-17. F. '60. Part time job opportunities for women. J. L. Meredith.

Occupational Outlook Quarterly. 4:9-16. D. '60. Training women and girls for work. J. A. Wells.

Occupational Outlook Quarterly. 4:29. D. '60. Federal pay rates and career examinations.

Occupational Outlook Quarterly. 5:15-22. My. '61. White-collar worker in the twentieth century. Carol Barry.

Occupational Outlook Quarterly. 5:18-25. S. '61. High school graduates and dropouts in the labor market, October 1960. Sophia Cooper.

Reader's Digest. 73:124-6+. Jl. '58. Help wanted: skilled blue-collar workers. J. P. Mitchell.

Reporter. 12:12-18. Ap. 7, '55. Age of the thinking robot and what it will mean to us. Robert Bendiner.

Reporter. 21:16-21. J. 23, '59. Negro worker asserts his rights. Paul Jacobs.

Senior Scholastic. 76:6-7. F. 10, '60. Job outlook for the 1960's. J. P. Mitchell.

*Senior Scholastic. 76:11-13. F. 10, '60. Military service as a career. S. F. Giffin.

U.S. News & World Report. 48:68-71. Ja. 11, '60. Best jobs of the future: a guide for your teen-agers.

III. MARRIAGE

Books and Pamphlets

*Black, A. D. If I marry outside my religion. (Public Affairs Pamphlet no 204) Public Affairs Committee. 22 E. 38th St. New York 16. '54.

Blood, R. O. Jr. and Wolfe, D. M. Husbands and wives. Free Press. New York. '60.

Bossard, J. H. S. and Boll, E. S. One marriage, two faiths. Ronald. New York. '57.

*Bowman, Henry. Marriage for moderns. McGraw. New York. '60.

Cavan, R. S. American marriage. Crowell. New York. '59.

*Landis, J. T. and Landis, M. G. Building a successful marriage. Prentice Hall. Englewood Cliffs, N.J. '58.

Mace, D. R. Success in marriage. Abingdon Press. Nashville. '58.

Mace, D. R. What is marriage counseling? (Public Affairs Pamphlet no 250) Public Affairs Committee. 22 E. 38th St. New York 16. '57.

Mead, Margaret. Male and female. (Mentor Book) New American Library. New York. '55. (Original ed.: Morrow. New York. '49)
Two sexes in contemporary America. p 184-285.

Riesman, David. Lonely crowd. Doubleday. Garden City, N.Y. '53.

Periodicals

Changing Times. 8:39-42. Je. '54. Family budget: how to set it up.

Changing Times. 11:7-13. F. '57. How much should you spend on what?

Changing Times. 11:21-6. Ap. '57. Should you invest for income?

Changing Times. 12:7-12. Je. '58. Money talk for young folks.

Collier's. 128:18-19+. N. 24, '51. What you should know about women—even if you're a woman. J. T. and M. G. Landis.

*Collier's. 134:34-6+. O. 1, '54. How to get along with any in-law. E. M. Duvall.
Adapted from a chapter in In-laws: pro and con. Association Press. New York. '54.

Coronet. 49:118-23. F. '61. Tragic trap of teenage marriage. David Landman.

Cosmopolitan. 142:24-32. Mr. '57. Money and your marriage. R. L. Heilbroner.

Editorial Research Reports. 11:381-98. My. 24, '61. Mixed marriage. H. B. Shaffer.

*Eugenics Quarterly. 1:254-60. D. '54. Changes in American marriage patterns and the role of women. N. N. Foote.

*Family Life Coordinator. 5:54-63. D. '56. Married undergraduates on the campus: an appraisal. L. A. Kirkendall.
Same in Cavan, R. S. ed. Marriage and family in the modern world. Crowell. New York. '60. p 261-8.

Good Housekeeping. 149:62-3+. Jl. '59. Risks you take in interfaith marriage. Carl Bakal.
Life. 41:108-16+. D. 24, '56. Changing roles in modern marriage. Robert Coughlan.
Life. 51:114-15+. S. 15, '61. Modern courtship: the great illusion. Ernest Havemann.
McCall's. 81:52+. S. '54. In-law trouble. Reuben Hill.
McCall's. 82:53+. Ap. '55. First years of marriage are crucial years; interview with Karl Menninger. Elizabeth Pope.
McCall's. 87:88-9+. N. '59. Why teen-age marriages are falling apart. Samuel Grafton.
McCall's. 88:122-3. F. '61. Secret marriage. D. R. Mace.
Marriage and Family Living. 18:29. F. '56. More working wives than ever.
Marriage and Family Living. 18:128-36. My. '56. Attitudes and policies concerning marriages among high school students. J. T. Landis.
*Marriage and Family Living. 19:227-33. Ag. '57. New burdens of masculinity. H. M. Hacker.
Marriage and Family Living. 20:278-82. Ag. '58. Family woman's expanding role. A. K. Leopold.
Marriage and Family Living. 20:293-5. Ag. '58. Study of high school marriages. R. S. Cavan and Grace Beling.
Nation. 177:348-50. O. 31, '53. Modern marriage: the danger point. Margaret Mead.
New York Times Magazine. p 11+. F. 10, '57. American men in a woman's world. Margaret Mead.
New York Times Magazine. p 59+. Ap. 5, '59. Campus marriages—for better or for worse. J. H. S. Bossard and E. S. Boll.
Social Forces. 39:116-25. D. '60. Campus values in mate selection. Robert McGinnis.
Today's Health. 37:19-21+. Mr. '59. Six ways to strengthen your marriage. Howard Whitman.
Today's Health. 38:40-1+. Ja. '60. How working mothers solve problems at home. M. K. Bersin.
*U.S. News & World Report. 48:80-5. Je. 6, '60. New look at early marriages; interview with Margaret Mead.

IV. PRESENT TRENDS

Books and Pamphlets

Butz, Otto. Unsilent generation. Rinehart. New York. '58.
Coleman, J. S. Adolescent society. Free Press. New York. '61.
Ginzberg, Eli. Values and ideals of American youth. Columbia University Press. New York. '61.
Goldsen, R. K. and others. What college students think. Van Nostrand. Princeton, N.J. '60.

Goodman, Paul. Growing up absurd; problems of youth in the organized system. Random House. New York. '60.

Habein, M. L. ed. Spotlight on the college student. American Council on Education. 1785 Massachusetts Ave. N.W. Washington 6, D.C. '59.

Hoopes, Roy. Complete Peace Corps guide. Dial. New York. '61.

Isaacs, H. I. Emergent Americans: a report on Crossroads Africa. John Day. New York. '62.

*Kennedy, J. F. Permanent Peace Corps; message to Congress, March 1, 1961. (H. Doc. no 98) United States. House of Representatives. 87th Congress, 1st session. Supt. of Docs. Washington 25, D.C. '61.
Same: Vital Speeches of the Day. 27:325-7. Mr. 15, '61.

Remmers, H. H. and Radler, D. H. American teenager. Bobbs-Merrill. Indianapolis. '57.

Ulich, Robert. Education of nations. Harvard University Press. Cambridge, Mass. '61.

United States. Peace Corps. Peace Corps fact book. The Corps. Washington 25, D.C. '61.

Periodicals

Atlantic Monthly. 207:40-4. F. '61. Pressures on college girls today. Carl Binger.

*Atlantic Monthly. 207:39-45. Ap. '61. Where is the college generation headed? David Riesman.

Atlantic Monthly. 208:56-60. S. '61. Why freshmen fail. H. G. Ridlon.

Commonweal. 71:653-4. Mr. 11, '60. Lunch-counter protests. Richard Lamanna.

Commonweal. 72:146-8. My. 6, '60. Point Four youth corps. H. S. Reuss.

Commonweal. 74:74-6. Ap. 14, '61. YAF's are coming. William Dunphy.

Congressional Digest. 39:295-313. D. '60. Proposed Federal Youth Conservation Corps; with pro and con discussion.

Current. 1:15-18. My. '61. Younger generation: disquiet on the student left. L. S. Feuer.

Editorial Research Reports. 2:913-29. D. 11, '57. Student movements. W. R. McIntyre.

Harper's Magazine. 219:76-9. N. '59. Why today's teen-agers seem so different. Eugene Gilbert.

Harper's Magazine. 222:73-7. My. '61. America's wandering scholars. R. M. Gummere, Jr.

Harper's Magazine. 223:63-8. S. '61. Peace Corps' secret mission. Benjamin De Mott.

Harper's Magazine. 223:129-82. O. '61. College scene [entire supplement].

Look. 25:16-25. Ja. 3, '61. Explosive generation. G. B. Leonard, Jr.
Mademoiselle. 51:260-1+. Ag. '60. Search for identity in college. H. M. Lynd.
*Mademoiselle. 53:236-9+. Ag. '61. Who are the student boat-rockers? Thomas Hayden.
Mademoiselle. 53:276+. Ag. '61. Cautious crusaders. M. A. Guitar.
Nation. 188:447-8. My. 16, '59. Tension beneath apathy: the teen-age ulcer. W. G. Cole.
Nation. 189:249-51. O. 24, '59. ROTC: failure of a mission. G. M. Lyons.
Nation. 189:395-7. N. 28, '59. Campus rebels find a cause. Allan Brick.
Nation. 192:451-60+. My. 27, '61. Campus report no. 4; rebels with a hundred causes.
Nation. 193:26-8. Jl. 15, '61. San Francisco-Moscow: why they walk. Barbara Deming.
National Review. 10:188. Mr. 25, '61. What about the Peace Corps? David Franke.
New Republic. 142:3-4. Mr. 14, '60. We are not afraid.
New Republic. 142:13-16. Ap. 25, '60. We are all so very happy. Helen Fuller.
New Republic. 142:14-16. My. 2, '60. Southern students take over. Helen Fuller.
New Republic. 143:14-15. O. 3, '60. Politics is for other people. Christopher Jencks.
New University Thought. 1:75-8. Spring '61. Student peace groups.
*New York Times. p E8. Mr. 12, '61. ABC of the Peace Corps. Peter Braestrup.
New York Times. p 18. D. 31, '61. 530 now abroad for Peace Corps.
*New York Times. p E5. Ja. 14, '62. Peace Corps finds it is in demand. Peter Braestrup.
New York Times Magazine. p 11+. My. 1, '60. Young Negro is a new Negro. Hodding Carter.
New York Times Magazine. p 5+. Ja. 29, '61. New young are now heard. Harold Taylor.
*New York Times Magazine. p 26+. F. 5, '61. Force of youth as a force for peace. Gertrude Samuels.
*New York Times Magazine. p 27+. Mr. 19, '61. Teen-age tyranny extends its empire. Grace Hechinger and F. M. Hechinger.
New York Times Magazine. p 25+. S. 10, '61. Time for freedom has come. M. L. King, Jr.
New York Times Magazine. p 26+. N. 19, '61. Negro education, for what? Gene Roberts, Jr.
New Yorker. 37:100+. Ap. 15, '61. Reporter at large: it doesn't seem quick to me. K. T. Kinkead.
Newsweek. 57:100. Mr. 13, '61. Youth turns to the right. Raymond Moley.
Occupational Outlook Quarterly. 5:11-15. S. '61. Opportunities for service in the Peace Corps. R. S. Bryan.

*Reporter. 24:20-3. Ja. 5, '61. Strategy of a sit-in. C. E. Lincoln.
Saturday Evening Post. 233:31+. S. 10, '60. Why do they misbehave. E. T. Hall.
Saturday Review. 43:28. D. 24, '60. Is a national Peace Corps enough? Youth cadres for peace. George Fersh.
Time. 77:34+. F. 10, '61. Campus conservatives.
Today's Health. 37:21+. Ap. '59. Why they quit college. Theodore Irwin.
U.S. News & World Report. 48:41-5. Mr. 14, '60. Will Negroes win in the South?
U.S. News & World Report. 50:44-5. Mr. 13, '61. ABC of Kennedy's Peace Corps.
Vital Speeches of the Day. 26:57-60. N. 1, '59. Youth and the open future. M. C. Patterson.